1 MONTH OF
FREE
READING

at

www.ForgottenBooks.com

By purchasing this book you are eligible for one month membership to ForgottenBooks.com, giving you unlimited access to our entire collection of over 1,000,000 titles via our web site and mobile apps.

To claim your free month visit:

www.forgottenbooks.com/free96617

ISBN 978-1-5284-7313-2
PIBN 10096617

PHARAIS A ROMANCE OF THE
ISLES BY FIONA MACLEOD

PRINTED BY HARPUR AND MURRAY
AT THE MORAY PRESS IN DERB·
MAY 180   AND SOLD BY FRANK
MURRAY AT HIS BOOKSHOPS IN
DERBY LEICESTER AND NOTTINGHAM

"*Mithich domh triall gu tigh Pharais.*"
(It is time for me to go up unto the House of Paradise.)
Muireadhach Albannach.

"*How many beautiful things have come to us from Pharais.*"
"Bileag-na-Toscùil."

To

E. W. R.

*Dear friend,—While you gratify me by your
pleasure in this inscription, you modestly depre-
cate the dedication to you of this story of alien
life—of that unfamiliar island-life so alien in
all ways from the life of cities, and, let me add,
from that of the great mass of the nation to
which, in the communal sense, we both belong.
But in the Domhan-Tòir of friendship there
are resting-places where all barriers of race,
training, and circumstance fall away in dust.
At one of these places of peace we met, a long
while ago, and found that we loved the same
things, and in the same way. You have been
in the charmed West yourself: have seen the
gloom and shine of the mountains that throw
their shadow on the sea: have heard the wave
whisper along that haunted shore which none
loves save with passion, and none, loving, can
bear to be long parted from. You, unlike so
many who delight only in the magic of sunshine
and cloud, love this dear land when the mists
drive across the hillsides, and the brown tor-
rents are in spate, and the rain and the black
wind make a gloom upon every loch, and fill
with the dusk of storm every strath, and glen,
and corrie. Not otherwise can one love it*

vii.

aright: " Tir nam Beann s'nan gleann' s'nan ghaisgach," *as one of our ancient poets calls it* —" *The land of hills, and glens, and heroes.*" *You, too, like Deirdre of old, have looked back on* "*Alba,*" *and, finding it passing fair and dear, have, with the Celtic Helen, said in your heart*—

> Inmain tir in tir ud fhoir,
> Alba cona lingantaibh ! . . .
> [" *Belovèd is that eastern land,*
> *Alba of the lochs.*"]

In the mythology of the Gael are three for-gotten deities, children of Delbaith-Dana. These are Seithoir, Teithoir, and Keithoir. One dwells. throughout the. sea, and beneath the soles of the feet of another are the highest clouds ; and these two may be held sacred for the beauty they weave for the joy of eye and ear. But now that, as surely none may gainsay, Keithoir is blind and weary, let us worship at his fane rather than give all our homage to the others. For Keithoir is the god of the earth ; dark-eyed, shadowy brother of Pan ; and his fane is among the lonely glens and mountains and lonelier isles of "Alba cona lingantaibh." *It is because you and I are of the children of Keithoir that I wished to grace my book with your name.*

The most nature-wrought of the English poets hoped he was not too late in transmuting into his own verse something of the beautiful mythology of Greece. But while Keats spun from the inexhaustible loom of genius, and I am but an obscure chronicler of obscure things, is it too presumptuous of me to hope that here, and mayhap elsewhere, I, the latest comer among older and worthier celebrants and co-enthusiasts, likewise may do something, howsoever little, to win a further measure of heed for, and more intimate sympathy with, that old charm and stellar beauty of Celtic thought and imagination, now, alas, like so many other lovely things, growing more and more remote, discoverable seldom in books, and elusive amid the sayings and oral legends and fragmentary songs of a passing race?

A passing race: and yet, mayhap not so. Change is inevitable; and even if we could hear the wind blowing along Magh Mell—the Plain of Honey—we might list to a new note, bitter-sweet: and, doubtless, the waves falling over the green roof of Tir-na-Thonn' murmur drowsily of a shifting of the veils of circumstance, which Keithoir weaves blindly in his dark place. But what was, surely is; and what is, surely may yet be. The form changes; the essential abides. As the saying goes among the islefolk: The shadow fleets beneath the cloud driven by the wind, and the cloud falls in rain or is sucked of the sun, but the wind sways this way and that for ever. It may well be that the Celtic Dream is not doomed to become a memory merely. Were it so, there would be less joy in all Springs to come, less hope in all brown Autumns; and the cold of a deathlier chill in all Winters still dreaming by the Pole. For the Celtic joy in the life of Nature—the Celtic vision—is a thing apart: it is a passion ; a visionary rapture. There is none like it among the peoples of our race.

Meanwhile, there are a few remote spots, as yet inviolate. Here, Anima Celtica still lives and breathes and hath her being. She dreams ; but if she awake, it may not necessarily be to a deepening twilight, or to a forlorn passage to Tir Tairngire—that Land of Promise whose borders shine with the loveliness of all forfeited, or lost, or banished dreams and realities of Beauty. It may be that she will arise to a wider sway, over a disfrontiered realm. Blue are the hills that are far from us. Dear saying of the Gael, whose soul as well as whose heart speaks therein. Far hills, recede, recede ! Dim veils of blue, woven from within and without, haunt us, allure us, always, always !

But now, before I send you my last word of greeting, let me add (rather for other readers than for you, who already know of them) a word concerning the Gaelic runes interpolated in Pharais.*

The "Urnuigh Smalaidh Teine" (p. 50) and "Altachadh Leapa" (p. 52) — respectively a prayer to be said at covering up the peat-fire at bed-time and a Rest-blessing—are relics of ancient Celtic folklore which were sent to the Rev. Dr. Alexander Stewart, of "Nether

---

* A slightly anglicised lection of the Gaelic word Pàras = Paradise, Heaven. " Pharais," properly, is the genitive and dative case of Pàras, as in the line from Muireadhach Albannach, quoted after the title page, " Mithich domh triall gu tigh Pharais"— "It is time for me to go up unto the House of Paradise."

Lochaber" fame, by Mr. A. A. Carmichael, of South Uist, who took them down from the recitation of a man living at Iocar of Uist. From the same Hebridean source came the "Rann Buachailleachd," or rune to be said over cattle when led to pasture at morn, introduced at p. 59. The English versions, by Dr. Stewart, appeared first in " The Inverness Courier," over twenty years ago. There are several versions current of the authentic incident of the innocent old woman held to be a witch, and of her prayer. I weave into my story the episode as I heard it many years ago, though with the rune rescued from oblivion by Dr. Stewart, rather than with the longer and commonly corrupted version still to be heard by the croft-fire in many localities, all " the far cry" from the Ord of Sutherland to the Rhinns of Islay. The " Laoidh Mhnathan "—the Chant of Women, at p. 117—is not ancient in the actual form here given, which is from an unpublished volume of " Oràin' Spioradail."

The sweetest-voiced of the younger Irish singers of to-day has spoken of the Celtic Twilight. A twilight it is; but, if night follow gloaming, so also does dawn succeed night. Meanwhile, twilight voices are sweet, if faint and far, and linger lovingly in the ear.

There is another Pàras than that seen of Alastair of Innisròn—the Tir-na-h'Oigh of friendship. Therein we both have seen beautiful visions and dreamed dreams. Take, then, out of my heart, this book of vision and dream.

FIONA MACLEOD.

"O bileag-geal,
O bileag-na-Toscùil, bileag Pharais,
O tha e boidheach !
Tha e boidheach !"

IT was midway in the seventh month of her great joy that the child moved, while a rapture leaped to her heart, within the womb of Lora, daughter of the dead Norman Maclean, minister of Innisròn, in the Outer Isles.

On the same eve the cruel sorrow came to her that had lain waiting in the dark place beyond the sunrise.

Alastair, her so dearly beloved, had gone, three days earlier, by the Western Isles steamer to the port of Greenock, thence to fare to Glasgow, to learn from a great professor of medicine concerning that which so troubled him—both by reason of what the islesmen whispered among themselves, and for what he felt of his own secret pain and apprehension.

There was a rocky spur on Innisròn whence the watcher could scan the headland round which the *Clansman* would come on her thrice - weekly voyage : in summer, while the isles were still steeped in the yellow shine; in autumn, when the sky seaward was purple, and every boulder in each islet was as transparent amber amid a vapour of amethyst rising from bases and hollow caverns of a cold day-dawn blue.

Hither Lora had come in the wane of the afternoon. The airs were as gentle and of as sweet balmy breath as though it were Summersleep rather than only the extreme of May. The girl looked, shading her eyes, seaward ; and saw the blue of the midmost sky laid as a benediction upon the face of the deep, but paler by a little, as the darkest turquoise is pale beside the lightest sapphire. She lifted her eyes from the pearl-blue of the horizon to the heart of the zenith, and saw there the soul of Ocean gloriously arisen. Beneath the weedy slabs of rock whereon she stood, the green of the sea-moss lent a yellow gleam to the slow-waving dead-man's-hair which the tide laved to and fro sleepily, as though the bewitched cattle of Sheumais the seer were drowsing there unseen, known only of their waving tails, swinging silently as the bulls dreamed of the hill-pastures they should see no more. Yellow-green in the sunlit spaces as the sea-hair was, it was dark against the shifting green light of the water under the rocks, and till so far out as the moving blue encroached.

To Lora's right ran a curved inlet, ending in a pool fringed with dappled fronds of sea-fern, mare's-tails, and intricate bladder-wrack. In the clear hollow were visible the wave-worn stones at the bottom, many crowned with spreading anemones, with here and there a star-fish motionlessly agleam, or a cloud of vanishing shrimps above the patches of sand, or hermit crabs toiling cumbrously from perilous shelter to more sure havens. Looking down she saw herself, as though her wraith had suddenly crept therein and was waiting to whisper that which, once uttered and once heard, would mean disunion no more.

Slipping softly to her knees, she crouched over the pool. Long and dreamily she gazed into its depths. What was this phantasm, she wondered, that lay there in the green-gloom as though awaiting her? Was it, in truth, the real Lora, and she but the wraith?

How strangely expressionless was that pale face, looking upward with so straightforward a mien, yet with so stealthy an understanding, with dark abysmal eyes filled with secrecy and dread, if not, indeed, with something of menace.

A thrill of fear went to the girl's heart. A mass of shadow had suddenly obscured her image in the water. Her swift fancy suggested that her wraith had abruptly shrouded herself, fearful of revelation. The next moment she realised that her own wealth of dark hair had fallen down her neck and upon her shoulders—hair dusky as twilight, but interwrought with threads of bronze that, in the shine of fire or sun, made an evasive golden gleam.

She shuddered as she perceived the eyes of her other self intently watching her through that cloudy shadow. A breath came from the pool, salt and shrewd, and cold as though arisen from those sea-sepulchres whence the fish steal their scales of gold and silver. A thin voice was in her ears that was not the lap of the tide or the cluck of water gurgling in and out of holes and crannies.

With a startled gesture she shrank back.

" What is it ?   What is it ? " she

cried ; but the sound of her own awed voice broke the spell : and almost at the same moment an eddy of wind came circling over the rock-bastions of the isle, and, passing as a tremulous hand over the pool, ruffled it into a sudden silvery sheen.

With a blithe laugh, Lora rose to her feet. The sunlight dwelt about her as though she were the sweetest flower in that lost garden of Aodh the poet, where the streams are unspanned rainbows flowing to the skiey cauldrons below the four quarters, and where every white flower has at dusk a voice, a whisper, of surpassing sweetness.

" O Alastair, Alastair ! " she cried, " will the boat never be coming that is to bring you back to me ! "

Not a black spot anywhere, of wherry or steamer, caught the leaping gaze. Like a bird it moved across the sea, and found no object whereon to alight.

The *Clansman* was often late ; but her smoke could be seen across Dunmore Head nigh upon quarter of an hour before her prow combed the froth from the Sound.

With a sigh, the girl moved slowly back by the way she had come. Over and over, as she went, she sang, crooningly, lines from a sweet song of the Gael, *O, Till, a Leannain !*

As she passed a place of birchen undergrowth and tall bracken, she did not see an old man, seated, grey and motionless as a heron. He looked at her with the dull eyes of age, though there was pity in them and something of a bewildered awe.

"Aye," he muttered below his breath, " though ye sing for your dear one to return, ye know not what I know. Have I not had the vision of him with the mist growin' up an' up, an' seen the green grass turn to black mools at his feet ? "

Lora, unwitting, passed ; and he heard her voice wax and wane, as falling water in a glen where the baffled wind among the trees soughs now this way and now that :—

" *Mo chridhe-sa! 's tusa 'bhios truagh,*
'bhios truagh,
Mur pill is' 'thog oirre gu cluaidh, gu
cluaidh !"

She went past the boulder on the path that hid the clachan from view, and within a net-throw of which was the byre of Mrs. Maclean's cottage, where, since her father's death, she had dwelt.

A tall, gaunt, elderly woman, with hair of the ivory white of the snow-berry, was about to pass from behind

the byre with a burthen of fresh
bracken for Ian Maclean's bed—for
the old islesman abode by the way of
his fathers, and was content to sleep
on a deerskin spread upon fresh-
gathered fern—when she caught sight
of Lora. She stopped, and with an
eager glance looked at the girl : then
beyond, and finally seaward, with her
long, thin, brown arm at an angle, and
her hand curved over her eyes against
the glare of the water.

Silence was about her as a garment.
Every motion of her, even, suggested
a deep calm. Mrs. Maclean spoke
seldom, and when she said aught it
was in a low voice, sweet and serene,
but as though it came from a distance
and in the twilight. She was of the
shadow, as the islesmen say ; and
strangers thought her to be austere in
look and manner, though that was only
because she gazed long before she re-
plied to one foreign to her and her
life : having the Gaelic, too, so much
more natively than the English, that
oftentimes she had to translate the
one speech into the other nearer to
her : that, and also because the quiet
of the sea was upon her, as often with
hill-folk there is a hushed voice and
mien.

Lora knew what was in her mind,

when she saw her gaze go seaward and then sweep hither and thither like a hawk ere it settles.

"The boat is not yet in sight, Mary; she is late," she said simply : adding immediately, "I have come back to go up Cnoc-an-Iolair; from there I'll see the smoke of the *Clansman* sooner. She is often as late as this."

Mrs. Maclean looked compassionately at the girl.

"Mayhap the *Clansman* will not be coming this way at all to-night, Lora. She may be going by Kyle-na-Sith."

A flush came into Lora's face. Her eyes darkened, as a tarn under rain.

"And for why would she not be sailing this way to-night, when Alastair is coming home, and is to be here before sundown ? "

"He may have been unable to leave. If he does not come to-day, he will doubtless be here to-morrow."

"To-morrow ! O Mary, Mary, have you ever loved that you can speak like that ? Think what Alastair went away for ! Surely you do not know how the pain is at my heart ? "

"Truly, *mùirnean*. But it is not well to be sure of that which may easily happen otherwise."

"To-morrow, indeed ! Why, Mary, if the *Clansman* does not come by this

8

evening, and has gone as you say by Kyle-na-Sith, she will not be here again till the day *after* to-morrow ! "

" Alastair could come by the other way, by the Inverary boat, and thence by the herring-steamer from Dunmore, after he had reached it from Uan Point or by way of Craig-Sionnach."

" That may be, of course ; but I think not. I cannot believe the boat will not be here to-night."

Both stood motionless, with their hands shading their eyes, and looking across the wide Sound, where the tide bubbled and foamed against the slight easterly wind-drift. The late sunlight fell full upon them, working its miracle of gold here and there, and making the skin like a flower. The outline of each figure stood out darkly clear as against a screen of amber.

For a time neither spoke. At last, with a faint sigh, Mrs. Maclean turned.

" Did you see Ian on your way, *Lora-mo-ghràidh* ? "

" No."

" Do not have speech with the old man to-night, dear one. He is not himself."

" Has he had the sight again ? "

" Ay, Lora."

Again a silence fell. The girl stood moodily, with her eyes on the ground :

the elder watched her with a steadfast, questioning look.

"Mary!"

Mrs. Maclean made no reply, but her eyes brought Lora's there with the answer that was in them.

"Ian has never had the sight again upon . . . upon Alastair, has he?"

"How can I say, *Lora-gaolaiche?*"

"But do you know if he has? If you do not tell me, I will ask him."

"I asked him that only yester-morning. He shook his head."

"Do you believe he can foresee all that is to happen?"

"No. Those who have the vision do not read all that is in the future. Only God knows. They can see the thing of peril, ay, and the evil of accident, and even Death—and what is more, the nearness and sometimes the way of it. But no man sees more than this—unless, indeed, he has been to Tir-na-h'Oigh."

Mrs. Maclean spoke the last words almost in a whisper, and as though she said them in a dream.

"Unless he has been to Tir-na-h' Oigh, Mary?"

"So it is said. Our people believe that the Land of Eternal Youth lies far yonder across the sea; but Aodh, the poet, is right when he tells us that that land is lapped by no green waves such as we know here, and that those who go thither do so in sleep, or in vision, or when God has filled with dusk the house of the brain."

"And when a man has been to Tir-na-h' Oigh in sleep, or in dream, or in mind-dark, does he see there what shall soon happen here?"

"It is said."

"Has Ian been beyond the West?"

"No."

"Then what he sees when he has the sight upon him is not *beannaichte:* is not a thing out of heaven?"

"I cannot say. I think not."

"Mary, is it the truth you are now telling me?"

A troubled expression came into the woman's face, but she did not answer.

"And is it the truth, Mary, that Ian has not had the sight upon Alastair since he went away—that he did not have it last night or this morning?"

Lora leaned forward in her anxiety. She saw that in her companion's eyes which gave her the fear. But the next moment Mrs. Maclean smiled.

"I too have the sight, *Lora-ghaolach;* and shall I be telling you that which it will be giving you joy to hear?"

"Aye, surely, Mary!"

"Then I think you will soon be in

the arms of him you love "—and, with a low laugh, she pointed across the sea to where a film of blue-grey smoke rose over the ridge of Dunmore headland.

" Ah, the *Clansman !* " cried Lora, with a gasp of joy : and the next moment she was moving down the path again towards the little promontory.

The wind had risen slightly. The splash, splash, of the sunny green waves against each other, the lapping of the blue water upon the ledges to the east, the stealthy whisper where the emerald-green tide-flow slipped under the hollowed sandstone, the spurtle of the sea-wrack, the flashing fall and foam-send of the gannets, the cries of the gulls, the slap of wind as it came over the forehead of the isle and struck the sea a score of fathoms outward— all gave her a sense of happiness. The world seemed suddenly to have grown young. The exultant Celtic joy stood over against the brooding Celtic shadow, and believed the lances of the sunlight could keep at bay all the battalions of gloom.

The breeze was variable, for the weft of blue smoke which suddenly curled round the bend of Dunmore had its tresses blown seaward, though where Lora stood the wind came from the west, and even caused a white foam along the hither marge of the promontory.

With eager eyes she watched the vessel round the point. After all, it was just possible she might not be the *Clansman*.

But the last sunglow shone full against Dunmore and upon the bows of the steamer as she swung to the helm ; and the moment the red funnel changed from a dusky russet into a flame of red, Lora's new anxiety was assuaged. She knew every line of the boat, and already she felt Alastair's kisses on her lips. The usual long summer-gloaming darkened swiftly— for faint films of coming change were being woven across the span of the sky from mainland oceanward. Even as the watcher on Innisròn stood, leaning forward in her eager outlook, she saw the extréme of the light lift upward as though it were the indrawn shaft of a fan. The contours of the steamer grew confused : a velvety duskiness overspread Dunmore foreland.

The sky overhead had become a vast lift of perishing yellow—a spent wave of daffodil by the north and by the south ; westward, of lemon, deepening into a luminous orange glow shot with gold and crimson, and rising as an exhalation from hollow cloud-sepulchres of amethyst, straits of scarlet, and immeasurable spaces of dove-grey filled with shallows of the most pale sea-green.

Lora stood as though wrought in marble. She had seen that which made the blood leap from her heart, and surge in her ears, and clamour against her brain.

No pennon flew at the peak of the steamer's foremast. This meant there was neither passenger nor freight to be landed at Innisròn, so that there was no need for the ferry.

She could scarcely believe it possible that the *Clansman* could come, after all, and yet not bring Alastair back to her. It seemed absurd : some ill-timed by-play; nay, a wanton cruelty. There must be some mistake, she thought, as she peered hungrily into the sea-dusk.

Surely the steamer was heading too much to the northward ! With a cry, Lora instinctively stretched her arms towards the distant vessel ; but no sound came from her lips, for at that moment a spurt of yellow flame rent the grey gloom, as a lantern was swung aloft to the mast-head.

In a few seconds she would know

all; for whenever the *Clansman* was too late for her flag-signal to be easily seen, she showed a green light a foot or so beneath the yellow.

Lora heard the heavy pulse of the engines, the churn of the beaten waves, even the delirious surge and suction as the spent water was driven along the hull and poured over and against the helm ere it was swept into the wake that glimmered white as a snow-wreath. So wrought was she that, at the same time, she was keenly conscious of the rapid *tweet-tweet-tweet-tweet-tweet—o-o-h sweet!—sweet!* of a yellowhammer among the whin close by, and of the strange, mournful cry of an oyster-opener as it flew with devious swoops towards some twilight eyrie.

The throb of the engines—the churn of the beaten waves—the sough of the swirling yeast—ever the churning, swirling, under-tumult, and through it and over it the heavy pulse, the deep panting rhythmic throb : this she heard, as it were the wrought surge of her own blood.

Would the green light never swing up to that yellow beacon?

A minute passed : two minutes : three! It was clear that the steamer had no need to call at Innisròn. She was coming up the mid of the Sound, and, unless the ferry-light signalled to her to draw near, she would keep her course north-westward.

Suddenly Lora realised this. At the same time there flashed into her mind the idea that perhaps Alastair was on board after all, but that he was ill, and had forgotten to tell the captain of his wish to land by the island ferry.

She turned, and, forgetful or heedless of her condition, moved swiftly from ledge to ledge, and thence by the path to where, in the cove beyond the clachan, the ferry-boat lay on the tide-swell, moored by a rope fastened to an iron clank fixt in a boulder.

"Ian! Ian!" she cried, as she neared the cove; but at first she saw no one, save Mrs. Maclean, black against the fire-glow from her cottage. "Ian! Ian!"

A dark figure rose from beside the ferry-shed.

"Is that you, Ian? *Am bheil am bhàta deas?* Is the boat ready? *Bi ealamh! bi ealamh! mach am bhàta:* quick! quick! out with the boat!"

In her eager haste she spoke both in the Gaelic and the English: nor did she notice that the old man did not answer her, or make any sign of doing as she bade him.

"*Oh, Ian, bi ealamh! bi ealamh! Faigh am bhàta deas! rach a stigh do'n bhàta!*"

Word for word, as is the wont of the people, he answered her :—

"Why is it that I should be quick? Why should I be getting the boat ready? For what should I be going into the boat?"

"The *Clansman!* Do you not see her? *Bi ealamh! bi ealamh!* or she will go past us like a dream."

"She has flown no flag, she has no green light at the mast. No one will be coming ashore, and no freight ; and there is no freight to go from here, and no one who wants the ferry unless it be yourself, *Lora nighean Tormaid!*"

"Alastair is there : he was to come by the steamer to-day ! Be quick, Ian ! Do you hear me?"

"I hear," said the old man, as he slowly moved towards the boulder to his left, unloosed the rope from the iron clank, and drew the boat into the deep water alongside the landing-ledge.

"There is no good in going out, *Lora bhàn!* The wind is rising : ay, I tell you, the wind goes high : we may soon hear the howling of the sea-dogs."

But Lora, taking no notice, had sprung into the boat, and was already adjusting the long oars to the old-fashioned wooden thole-pins. Ian followed, grumblingly repeating, "*Tha gaoth ruhòr am! Tha coltas stairm' air!*"

Once, however, that the wash of the sea caught the wherry, and the shrewd air sent the salt against their faces, the old man appeared to realise that the girl was in earnest. Standing, he laid hold of the sloped mast, to steady himself against the swaying as the tide sucked at the keel and the short waves slapped against the bows, and then gave a quick calculating glance seaward and at the advancing steamer.

Rapidly he gave his directions to Lora to take the helm and to keep the boat to windward :—

"*Gabh an stiuir, Lora : cum ris a' ghàoith i !*"

The next moment the long oars were moving slowly, but powerfully, through the water, and the ferry-boat drove into the open, and there lay over a little with the double swing of wind and tide.

The gloaming was now heavy upon the sea ; for a mist had come up with the dipping of the sun, and thickened the dusk.

Suddenly Ian called to Lora to hold the oars. As soon as she had caught them, and was steadying the boat in the cross surge of the water, he lifted a lantern from under the narrow foredeck, lighted the wick below the seat (after the wind had twice blown the flame into the dark), and then, gripping the mast, waved the signal to and fro overhead.

It was well he thought of this, for the steamer was going at full speed, and would not have slackened.

In a few minutes thereafter, the heavy stertorous throb and splash was close by them, while the screw revolved now at quarter-speed.

A hoarse voice came from the *Clansman :*

" Ferry ahoy ! "

" Ay, ay, ta ferry she will pe," called back Ian in the quaint English of which he was so proud : though he thought the language a poor, thin speech, and fit only for folk who never left the mainland.

"What are ye oot for, Ian ? Ha' ye ony body comin' aboard ? "

" We've come out for Mr. Alastair Macleod," Lora broke in eagerly : " we've come to take him off."

" Hoots, my girl, what for d' ye fash yersel an' us too for the like o' sic havers. There's no one aboard who wants to land at Innisròn : an' as for Alastair Macleod, he wasna' on the *Clansman* when we left Greenock, so he couldna' well be on her the now !

As for you, Ian Maclean, are ye doited, when, wi' neither flag nor green light aloft, ye stop the steamer like this, a' for a lassie's haverin'! Ye'll hear o' this yet, my man, I'se telling ye! Auld fule that ye are, awa' wi' ye! keep aff the wash o' the steamer: . . . an' by the Lord I'll . . ."

But already the *Clansman* was forging ahead, and the second-officer's menace was swallowed up in the tumult of churned seas.

A minute later the steamer was a dark mass to the nor'-west, with a sheet of white writhing after her, and a swirl of flaming cinders from her funnel riding down the night like a shoal of witch-lights.

The wherry rocked heavily, caught as she was in the surge from the screw, and lying adrift in the sliding hollows and rough criss-cross of the waves.

Lora sat motionless and speechless. The old man stared down into the darkness of the boat: but though his lips moved continuously, no sound came from them.

For a time it was as though a derelict were the sport of the sea, which had a dull moan in it, that partly was from the stifled voice of the tide as it forced its way from the cauldrons of the deep, and partly from the fugitive clamour of breaking waves, and mostly from the now muffled, now loud and raucous sough of the wind as it swung low by the surge, or trailed off above the highest reach of the flying scud.

At last, in a whisper, the girl spoke.

" Ian, has aught of evil come to Alastair ? "

" God forbid ! "

" Do you know anything to his undoing ? "

" No, Lora bhàn."

" You have not had the sight upon him lately ? "

The islesman hesitated a moment. Raising his eyes at last, he glanced first at his companion and then out into the dusk across the waves, as though he expected to see some one or something there in answer to his quest.

" I dreamt a dream, Lora, wife of Alastair. I saw you and him and another go away into a strange place. You and the other were as shadows ; but Alastair was a man, as now, though he walked through mist, and I saw nothing of him but from the waist upward."

Silence followed this, save for the wash of the sea, the moan of wind athwart wave, and the soft rush of the breeze overhead.

Ian rose, and made as though he

were going to put out the oars; but as he saw how far the boat had drifted from the shore, and what a jumble of water lay between them and the isle, he busied himself with hoisting the patched brown sail.

As if no interval had occurred, Lora abruptly called him by name.

" Ian," she added, " what does the mist mean ? . . . the mist that you saw about the feet and up to the waist of Alastair ? "

There was no reply. Ian let go the sail, secured it, and then seated himself a few feet away from Lora.

She repeated the question : but the old man was obstinately silent, nor did he speak word of any kind till the wherry suddenly slackened, as she slipped under the lee of the little promontory of the landing-place.

" The tide will be on turning now," he exclaimed in his awkward English, chosen at the moment because he did not dare to speak in the Gaelic, fearful as he was of having any further word with his companion ; " and see, after all, the wind she will soon pe gone."

Lora, who had mechanically steered the boat to its haven, still sat in the stern, though Ian had stepped on to the ledge and was holding the gunwhale close to it so that she might step ashore with ease. She looked at him as though she did not understand. The old man shifted uneasily. Then his conscience smote him for having used the cold, unfriendly English instead of the Gaelic so dear to them both: for was not the girl in the shadow of trouble, and did he not foresee for her more trouble to come? So, in a gentle, apologetic voice, he repeated in Gaelic what he had said about the tide and the wind :—

"*Thill an sruth: Dh' fhalbh a' ghàoth.*"

"There will be peace to-night," he added. "It was but a sunset breeze, after all. There will be no storm. I think now there will be a calm. It will be bad for the herring-boats. It is a long pull and a hard pull when the water sleeps against the keel. A dark night, too, most likely."

Lora rose, and slowly stepped on shore. She took no notice of Ian's sudden garrulity. She did not seem to see him even.

He looked at her with momentary resentment: but almost simultaneously a pitiful light came into his eyes.

"He will be to-morrow," he murmured, "and if not, then next day for sure."

Lora moved up the ledge in silence.

In the middle of the cove she stopped, waved her hand, and, in a dull voice bidding good night, wished sound sleep to him :—

"*Beannachd leibh! Cadal math dhiubh!*"

Ian answered simply, "*Beannachd leibh!*" and turned to fasten the rope to the iron clank.

The dew was heavy, even on the rough salt spear-grass which fringed the sand above the cove. On the short sheep-grass, on the rocky soil beyond, it was dense, and shone white as a shroud in a dark room. A bat swung this way and that, whirling silently. The fall of the wind still sighed in the bent rowan trees to the west of the clachan, where the pathway diverged from the shore. Against the bluff of Cnoc-an-Iolair it swelled intermittently : its voice in the hollows and crevices of the crag broken up in moans and short gasps, fainter and fainter.

Lora noted all this wearily as she advanced. She was conscious, also, of the nibbling of the sheep, quenching their thirst with the wet grass : of the faint swish of her feet going through the dew : of the dark track, like a crack in black ice, made wherever she walked in the glisten. But though she saw and unwittingly noted, her

24

thoughts were all with Alastair and with what had kept him.

In her remote life there was scarce room for merely ordinary vicissitudes. It was not a thing to ponder as ominous that one should go out to sea after herring or mackerel and not return that night or the morrow, or even by the next gloaming, or second dawn ; or that a man should go up among the hills and not come back for long after his expected hour. But that one could miss the great steamer was a thing scarce to believe in. To Lora, who had been so little on the mainland, and whose only first-hand knowledge of the feverish life of towns was derived from her one winter of school-life at Rothesay and brief visits to Greenock and Oban, it was difficult to realise how any one could fail to leave by the steamer, unless ill or prevented by some serious mischance. The periodical coming of the *Clansman* symbolised for her, to a certain extent, the inevitable march of time and fate. To go or come by that steam-driven, wind-heedless vessel was to be above the uncertainties and vicissitudes to which ordinary wayfaring mortals are subject. The girl thought she knew so much that to her all of what town-life meant must be bare, because of her reading :

knowing not that, with a woman whose heart aches, a tear will drown every word writ in any book, a sigh scatter the leaves into nothingness.

Deep was the puzzle to her as she slowly ascended the path which led to Mary Maclean's cottage. She stopped once or twice, half unconsciously, to smell the fragrance of the bog-myrtle where the gale grew in tufts out of the damper patches, or of the thyme as it was crushed under her feet and made over-sweet, over-poignant by the dew.

The peat-reek reached her nostrils from the cottage, blent with the breaths of the cows that still loitered afoot, munching the cool wilding fodder. Her gaze, too, fell upon the fire-lit interior, with a table overspread by a white cloth, flushed by the glow that wavered from betwixt the red-hot bars : and, later, upon the figure of Mrs. Maclean, who had come out to meet her, or, more likely, had been there ever since the ferry-boat had gone off upon its useless errand.

"Are you wet, Lora? Are you cold?" she asked, as the girl drew near. There was no need to say aught of the bitter disappointment, any more than to speak of the glooming of the dusk : both were obvious facts beyond the yea or nay of speech.

" I am very tired, Mary."

" Come in, dear, and have your tea. It will do you good. *Lora-mo-ghràidh*, you should not have gone out in the ferry-boat. It was no use, and the sea was rough, and you might have come to harm ; and what would Alastair Macleod be saying, to-morrow, if he found his heart's-delight ill, and that I had stood by and seen her do so foolish a thing ? "

" Oh, Mary, do you really think he will be here to-morrow ? "

" Surely."

" But I fear he will wait now till the next sailing of the *Clansman*."

" We cannot say. Come in, my fawn, out of the chill."

"It is going to be a lovely night. The wind falls fast : even now it is almost still. The purple peace will be upon everything to-night. I am restless : I do not wish to go in-doors."

" No, no, Lora dear to me ! Come in and have your tea, and then rest. You can rise at daybreak, if you will, and go round the island, lest he should be coming in any of the herring-smacks."

" I want to speak to Ian."

" Ian has gone across to Ivor Maquay's ; he will not be here to-night."

Lora looked suspiciously at the speaker. Had she not left Ian a few minutes ago, and was he not even now following her? She stared about her, but saw no one. In the gloaming she could just descry the black mass of the wherry. Ian was nowhere visible. She did not think of scrutinising the shadow of the beached and long disused coble which lay a few yards away. Had she done so, she might have perceived the old islesman standing rigid. He had overheard his kinswoman, and understood. As soon as the two women had entered the cottage, he moved swiftly and silently away, and, traversing the clachan, was soon swallowed up of the darkness.

After the meal was ended, Lora found herself overworn with excitement. All wish to go out again went from her. From where she lay resting, she watched Mrs. Maclean put away the things and then seat herself by the fire.

For a long time neither woman spoke. A drowsy peace abode upon the threshold.

The hot red glow of the peats shone steadily.

At first there had been a little lamp on the table, but after a time Mrs. Maclean had extinguished it. Instead, she had thrown upon the fire a log of pinewood. The dry crackle, the spurt of the sap as it simmered in the heat, the yellow tongues and sudden red fangs and blue flames, gave the sound and glow whereof a sweeter silence can be wrought into what has been but stillness before.

An hour went by. With brief snatches of talk, all made up of fears and hopes, another hour passed. Then a long quietness again, broken at the last by a low crooning song from the elder woman, as she leaned to the fire and stared absently into its heart. The song was old : older than the oldest things, save the summits of the mountains, the granite isles, and the brooding pain of the sea. Long ago it had been sung by wild Celtic voices, before ever spoken word was writ in letters—before that again, may-hap, and caught perhaps from a wailing Pictish mother—so ancient was the moving old-world strain, so antique the words of the lullaby that was dim with age when it soothed to sleep the child Ossian, son of Fingal.

When the crooning died away, Lora slept. With soft step Mrs. Maclean moved across the room, and lightly dropped a plaid over the girl's figure, recumbent in beautiful ease upon the low bed-couch.

She returned slowly to her place by the fire. After a while she was about to seat herself, when she started violently. Surely that was a face pressed for a moment against the window?

With a strange look in her eyes, she reproved herself for her nervous folly. She sat down, with gaze resolutely fixt on the glowing peats : nor would she have stirred again, but for a sound as of a low moan.

The blood ran chill in her veins ; her mouth twitched ; and the inter-twisted fingers of her hands were white and lifeless with the fierce grip that came of her fear.

But she was not a woman to be mastered by terror. With a quivering sigh she rose, looked round the room, forced herself to stare fixedly at the window, and then moved quietly to the door.

As soon as she felt the air upon her brows she became calm, and all dread left her.

"Is that you, Ian ?" she whispered.

There was no one visible : no sound.

"Is that you, Alastair Macleod ?"

So low was the utterance that, if any one had been there, he could scarce have heard it.

To her strained ears it was as though she heard a light susurrus of brushed dew : but it might be a wandering breath of air among the gale, or an adder moving through the grass, or a fern-owl hawking under the rowan-trees.

She waited a little; then, with a sigh of relief, re-entered the cottage and closed the door.

A glance at Lora showed her that the girl was sleeping unperturbed. For some time thereafter she sat by the fire, brooding over many things. Weary, at last, she rose, cast a farewell glance at the sleeper, and then slipt quietly to her bed in the adjoining room.

Night lay passively upon the sea, upon the isle, upon the clachan. Not a light lingered in any cottage, save the fire-glow in that of Mary Maclean : a hollow, attenuating beam that stared through the dark unwaveringly.

Neither star nor moon was visible. The clouds hung low, but without imminence of rain for the isles, drawn inland as the vapours were by the foreheads of the bens.

An hour later the door of the cottage opened and closed again, silently. It was Lora who came forth.

She walked hesitatingly at first, and then more swiftly, not pausing till she reached the little boulder-pier. There she stood motionless, listening intently.

The water lapped among the hollows, above which the ebb-left shellfish gaped thirstily. There was a lift among the dulse-heaps, as though a finger stirred them and let loose their keen salt smells. The bladder-wrack moved with strange noises, sometimes startlingly loud, oftenest as if sea-things were being stifled or strangled.

From the promontory came a cry: abrupt, strident—the hunger-note of a skua. The thin pipe of the dotterel fell into the darkness beyond the shallows where the sea-mist lay. In the Kyle a muffled, stertorous breath, near and twice as far away, told that two whales were in the wake of the mackerel.

From the isle, no sound. The sheep lay on the thyme, or among the bracken, still as white boulders. The kye crouched, with misty nostrils laid low to the damp grass, rough with tangled gale. The dogs were silent. Even the tufted canna hung straight and motionless. The white moths had, one by one, fallen like a falling feather. The wind-death lay · upon all : at the last, too, upon the sea.

II.

SLOWLY, as though a veil were withdrawn, the cloudy dusk passed from the lift. The moon, lying in violet shadow, grew golden: while the sheen of her pathway, trailed waveringly across the sea and athwart the isle, made Innisròn seem as a beautiful body motionlessly adrift on the deep.

One by one the stars came forth —solemn eyes watching for ever the white procession move onward orderly where there is neither height, nor depth, nor beginning, nor end.

In the vast stellar space the moon-glow waned until it grew cold, white, ineffably remote. Only upon our little dusky earth, upon our restless span of waters, the light descended in a tender warmth. Drifting upon the sea, it moved tremulously onward, weaving the dark waters into a weft of living beauty.

Strange murmur of ocean, even when deep calm prevails, and not the most homeless wind lifts a weary wing from wave-gulf to wave-gulf. As a voice heard in dream; as a whisper in the twilight of one's own soul; as a breath, as a sigh from one knows not whence, heard suddenly and with recognising awe; so is this obscure, troublous echo of a tumult that is over, that is not, but that may be, that awaiteth.

To Lora it was almost inaudible. Rather, her ears held no other sound than the babbling repetitive chime and whisper of the lip of the sea moving to and fro the pebbles on the narrow strand just beyond her.

Her eyes saw the lift of the dark, the lovely advance of the lunar twilight, the miracle of the yellow bloom— golden here and here white as frost-fire—upon sea and land : they saw, and yet saw not. Her ears heard the muffled voice of ocean and the sweet recurrent whispering of the foam-white runnels beside her : they heard, and yet heard not.

Surely, in the darkness, in the lone-liness, she would have knowledge of Alastair. Surely, she thought, he would come to her in the spirit. In deep love there is a living invisible line from soul to soul whereby portent of joy or disaster, or passion of loneliness, or passion of fear, or passion of longing may be conveyed with terrifying surety.

How beyond words dreadful was this remoteness which environed her, as the vast dome of night to a single white flower growing solitary in a waste place.

Inland upon the isle, seaward, skyward, Lora looked with aching eyes. The moonlight wounded her with its peace. The shimmering sea beat to a rhythm atune to a larger throb than that of a petty human life. In the starry infinitude her finitude was lost, absorbed, as a grain of sand windblown a few yards across an illimitable desert.

That passionate protest of the soul against the absolute unheed of nature was hers: that already defeated revolt of the whirling leaf against the soaring, far-come, far-going wind that knows nothing of what happens beneath it in the drift of its inevitable passage.

With a sob, she turned, vaguely yearning for the human peace that abode in the cottage. As she moved, she saw a shadow, solidly clear-cut in the moonlight, sweep from a rock close by, as though it were a swinging scythe.

Instinctively she glanced upward, to see if the cloud-counterpart were overhead.   The sky was now cloudless : neither passing vapour nor travelling wild-swan had made that shadow leap from the smooth boulder into the darkness.

She trembled : for she feared she had seen the Watcher of the Dead. At the wane of the last moon, an old islesman had passed into the white sleep.   Lora knew that his spirit would have to become the Watcher of Graves till such time as another soul should lapse into the silence.   Was this he, she wondered with instinctive dread— was this Fergus, weary of his vigil, errant about the isle which had been the world to him, a drifting shadow from graveyard to byre and sheiling, from fold to dark fold, from the clachan-end to the shore-pastures, from coble to havened coble, from the place of the boats to the ferry-rock?   Did he know that he would soon have one to take over from him his dreadful peace?   Or was he in no satiate peace, but an-hungered as a beast of prey for the death of another?   And then . . . and then . . . who was this other?   Who next upon the isle would be the Watcher of the Dead?

With a low, shuddering breath, she sighed, " *Fergus !*"

The fall of her voice through the

silence was an echo of terror. She clasped her hands across her breast. Her body swayed forward as a bulrush before the wind.

"*Ah, Dia! Dia!*" broke from her lips; for, beyond all doubt, she saw once again the moving of a darkness within the dark.

Yet what she saw was no shadow-man weary of last vigil, but something that for a moment filled her with the blindness of dread. Was it possible? Was she waylaid by one of those terrible dwellers in twilight-water of which she had heard so often from the tellers of old tales?

"*Toradh nu feudalach gun am faicinn,*" she muttered with cold lips: "the offspring of the cattle that have not been seen!"

"Ah, no, no!" she cried. The next moment, and with a sob of relief, she saw a moonbeam steal upon the hollow and reveal its quietude of dusk. She would have moved at once from boulder to boulder, eager for that lost sanctuary whence she had come—when the very pulse of her heart sprang to the burst of a human sob close by.

She stood still, as though frozen. A moment before, the breath from her lips was visible: now not the faintest vapour melted into the night-air.

Was she dreaming, she wondered, when the stifling grip at her heart had mercifully relaxed.

No : there was no mistake. Blent with the gurgle and cluck and whisper of the water among the lifted bladder-wrack and in and out of the pools and crannies in the rocks, there was the piteous sound of a human sob.

All at once, everything became clear to Lora. She knew that Alastair was near : she did not even dread that he was present as a disembodied spirit. He had reached the isle after all, but in some strange sorrow had not sought her straightway.

"*Alastair !*" she cried, yearningly.

No one answered ; no one stirred ; nothing moved. But the muffled sobbing was hushed.

"Alastair ! Alastair !"

Slowly from a sand-drift beside the ferry-rock a tall figure arose. For a few moments it stood motionless, black against the yellow shine of the moon. The face was pale ; that of a man, young, with the thin lips, the shadowy eyes that in sunlight would shine sea-blue, the high oval features, the tangled, curly, yellow-tawny hair of the islesmen of the ancient Suderöer, in whose veins the Celtic and the Scandinavian strains commingle.

Alastair was as visible as though he were in the noon-light.

Lora looked at him, speechless. She saw that in his strained eyes, in his wrought features, which told her he had drunken of sorrow. His dishevelled hair, his whole mien and appearance showed that he was in some dire extremity.

"*Alastair!*"

He heard the low, passionate appeal, but at first he did not stir. Then, and yet as though constrainedly and in weariness, he raised and stretched forth his arms.

Swift as a gliding shadow, Lora was beside him, and claspt to his heart.

For a time, neither spoke. His heart beat loud and heavily: against his breast her head lay, with her breath coming and going like a wounded bird panting in the green-gloom of the thicket.

" O Alastair, Alastair, what is it ? " she murmured at last, raising her head and looking into his pale, distraught face.

"What made you come out in the dark, Lora-mùirnean ? "

" I could not rest. I was too unhappy. I thought—I thought—no, I do not think I dared to believe that you might come to-night after all ; but something made me long to go down to the sea. Did you see me only now, dear heart?"

"No, Lora."

For a moment she was still, while she gazed fixedly at Alastair.

" Ah," she whispered at last, "then you have been here all this night, and I not knowing it! Ah, Alùinn, it was *your* heart crying to mine that made me rise and leave the cottage and come out into the dark. But why did you not come to me? When did you come to Innisròn? How did you come?"

" Dear, I could not wait for the *Clansman*. I left Greenock three hours earlier by the *Foam*, James Gilchrist's tug; for he undertook to put me ashore at the haven below Craig-Sionnach. Thence I walked to Dunmore. But I was not well, Lora; and I was so long on the way that I missed the *Clansman* as well as the Dunmore herring-steamer. Before nightfall, however, I persuaded Archibald Macleod, of Tighnacraigh, to bring me here on his smack. I landed at the Rock of the Seafolk. It was already dusk, and my heart was against yours in longing, my beautiful gloom : yet over me came such a sorrow that I could not bear the homing, and so moved restlessly from shadow to shadow. I felt as though it would be better for me to deal with my sorrow alone and in the night, and that it was more bearable since I was so near you, and that any moment I could go to you."

"Why, why did you not come, Alastair? Oh, I longed, longed for you so!"

"Once I came close to the cottage, almost happy since I knew that you were so near to me. The red glow that warmed the dark without comforted me. I thought I would look in upon you for a moment; and if you and Mary were awake and talking, that I should let you know I had come. But I saw that you lay in sleep; and I had scarce time to withdraw ere, as I feared, Mary saw me—though see me, indeed, perhaps she did, for in a brief while she opened the door and came out, and would have discovered me but that I moved swiftly to the shadow of the birk-shaws. Then, after a little, I wandered down by the shore. There was a voice in the sea— calling, calling. It was so cool and sweet: soft was the balm of the air of it, as the look of your eyes, Lora, as the touch of your hand. I was almost healed of my suffering, when suddenly the pain in my head sprang upon me, and I crouched in the hollow yonder, chill with the sweat of my agony."

"O Alastair, Alastair, then you are no better: that great doctor you went so far to see has done you no good?"

"And in the midst of my pain, Lora my Rest, I saw you standing by the sea upon the ferry-ledge. At first I took you for a vision, and my heart sank. But when the moonlight reached the isle and enfolded you, I saw that it was you indeed. And once more my pain and my sorrow overcame me."

"Alastair, I am terrified! It was not thus for you before you went away. Great as was your pain, you had not this gloom of sorrow. Oh, what is it, what is it, dear heart? Tell me, tell me!"

Slowly Alastair held Lora back from him, and looked long and searchingly into her eyes.

She shrank, in an apprehension that, like a bird, flew bewildered from the blinding light that flashed out of the darkness—a vain bewilderment of fore-doom.

Then, with a great effort, she bade him tell her what he had to say.

Too well he knew there was no time to lose: that any day, any moment, his dark hour would come upon him, and that then it would be too late. Yet he would fain have waited.

" Lora, have you heard aught said by any one concerning my illness ? "

" Dear, Father Manus told me, on the day you went away, that you feared the trouble which came upon your father, and upon your father's father ; and oh, Alastair my beloved, he told me what that trouble was."

" Then you know : you can understand ? "

" What ? "

" That which now appals me . . . now kills me."

" Alastair ! "

" Yes, Lora ? "

" Oh, Alastair, Alastair, you do not mean that . . . that . . . you too . . . *you* are . . . are . . . that *you* have the . . . the . . . mind-dark ? "

" Dear heart of mine, this sorrow has come to us. I —— "

With a sharp cry Lora held him to her, despairingly, wildly, as though even at that moment he were to be snatched from her. Then, in a passion of sobbing, she shook in his arms as a withered aspen-leaf ere it fall to the wind.

The tears ran down his face ; his mouth twitched ; his long, thin fingers moved restlessly in her hair and upon her quivering shoulder.

No other sound than her convulsive sobs, than his spasmodic breathing, met in the quietude of whisper-music exhaled as an odour by the sea and by the low wind among the corries and upon the grasses of the isle.

A white moth came fluttering slowly towards them, hovering vaguely awhile overhead, and then drifting alow and almost to their feet. In the shadow it loomed grey and formless—an obscure thing that might have come out of the heart or the unguarded brain. Upward again it fluttered, idly this way and that: then suddenly alit upon the hair of Alastair, poising itself on spread wings, and now all agleam as with pale phosphorescent fire, where the moonlight filled it with sheen as of white water falling against the sun.

The gleam caught Lora's eyes as, with a weary sigh, she lifted her head.

A strange smile came into her face. Slowly she disengaged her right arm, and half raised it. Alastair was about to speak, but her eyes brought silence upon him.

" *Hush !* " she whispered at last.

He saw that her eyes looked beyond his, beyond him as it seemed. What did she see? The trouble in his brain moved anew at this touch of mystery.

" What is it, Lora ? "

44

" Hush, hush ! . . . I see a sign
from heaven upon your forehead . . .
the sign of the white peace that Sheu-
mais says is upon them who are of the
company of the Belovëd."

" Lora, what are you saying ? What
is it ? What do you see ? "

His voice suddenly was harsh, fret-
ful. Lora shrank for a moment ; then,
as the white moth rose and fluttered
away into the dark, faintly agleam
with moonfire till it reached the sha-
dow, she pitifully raised her hand to
his brow.

" Come, dear, let us go in. All will
be well with us, whatever happens."

" Never . . . never . . . never!"

" O Alastair, if it be God's will ? "

" Ay, and if it be God's will ? "

" I cannot lose you : you will always
be mine : no sorrow can part us :
nothing can separate us : nothing but
the Passing, and that . . . . ."

" Lora ! "

For answer she looked into his eyes.

" Lora, it is of that, of the Passing :
. . . are you . . . are you brave
enough not only to endure . . .
but to . . . if we thought it well
. . . if I asked you . . ? "

A deep silence fell upon both.
Hardly did either breathe. By some
strange vagary of the strained mind,

Lora thought the throb of her heart against her side was like the pulse of the engines of the *Clansman* to which she had listened with such intent expectation that very evening.

From the darkness to the north came the low monotone of the sea, as a muffled voice prophesying through the gates of Sleep and Death. Far to the east the tide-race tore through the Sound with a confused muttering of haste and tumult. Upon the isle the wind moved as a thing in pain, or idly weary: lifting now from cranny to corrie, and through glen and hollow, and among the birk-shaws and the rowans, with long sighs and whispers where by Uisghe-dhu the valley of moonflowers sloped to the sea on the west, or among the reeds, and the gale, and the salt grasses around the clachan that lay duskily still on the little brae above the haven.

"Lora . . . would you . . . would . . ?"

Only her caught breath at intervals gave answer. The short lisp and gurgle of the water in the seaweed close by came nearer. The tide was on the flood, and the sand about their feet was already damp.

The immense semicircle of the sky domed sea and land with infinity. In the vast space the stars and planets fulfilled their ordered plan. Star by star, planet by planet, sun by sun, universe by universe moved jocund in the march of eternal death.

Beyond the two lonely figures, seaward, the moon swung, green-gold at the heart with circumambient flame of pearl.

Beautiful the suspended lamp of her glory : a censer swung before the Earth-Altar of the Unknown.

In their human pain the two drew closer still. The remote alien silences of the larger life around vaguely appalled them. Yet Lora knew what was in his thought : what he foreshadowed: what he wished.

"It shall be as you will, Alastair, heart of me, life of me," she whispered. Then, with clasping arms, and dear entreaty, she urged him homeward.

"Come, come home, Alastair, *Alùinn*. Enough of sorrow to-night. Speak to me to-morrow of all that is in your mind ; but to-night . . . to-night, no more ! My heart will break. Come, dearest. Come, *mo mùirnean!* Hark! the wind is crying in the corrie : it is rising again on the other side of the isle : and we are already chill — oh, cold, so cold ! "

Hand in hand, they moved slowly

upward along the little pathway of mingled grass and shingle which led to. the clachan from the ferry : he with bowed head, she with upward face.

A dog barked from a byre, another answered from a sheiling beyond. Suddenly there was a rushing sound, and Ghaoth, Alastair's dog, came leaping upon his master, whining and barking with joy. He stooped and fondled it ; but in vain tried to quell its ecstasy in seeing him again.

Whether aroused by the barking of Ghaoth, or having awoke and found Lora absent from the cottage, Mrs. Maclean had risen, lit a candle, and now stood upon the threshold, looking intently at the twain as they approached.

Among the islefolk many words are not used. The over-arching majesty of the sky, the surrounding majesty of the sea, the loneliness of these little windswept spots of earth isled in remote waters, leave a hush upon the brain, and foster eloquent silences rather than idle words.

Mrs. Maclean knew intuitively that something of disaster was in this nocturnal return of Alastair: that he and Lora had met by chance, or through a summons unknown to her : and that now they came—to her, in their youth, so tragically piteous under the shadow of calamity—craving only for that impossible boon of the young in sorrow : peace.

When they drew near to her, she turned and placed the candle on the table. Then, facing them, she came forward, led them in by the hand, and closed the door. She saw that Alastair was hatless, and his clothes damp and travel-stained; so with quiet, home-sweet words, she persuaded him to change his things while she laid some food for him to break his long fast with.

But though wearily he did the one, he would have nothing of the other save a draught of warm milk.

A heavy drowsiness was now upon him. He could scarce uplift the lids from his eyes. His voice, when he spoke at all, was so low that it was barely audible.

After a silence, during which he had looked long at the fire, and closed his eyes at the last, with Lora's gaze hungrily set upon him, and the dark, sweet gloom of Mrs. Maclean's, wet with the dew of unshed tears, upon both of the twain whom she loved so passing well, he murmured huskily and confusedly—

" By green pastures . . . I will lay me down to sleep. . . . . It calleth, calleth . . ."

Suddenly Mrs. Maclean arose. Taking Lora's hand, she led her to the fireside and motioned her to kneel beside Alastair. Then, blowing out the candle-flame, she too knelt. Only the fireglow now lit the room, filled with brooding shadows in the corners and with warm dusk where the two women kneeled and the man slept.   ·

With arms lifted as if in invocation, the elder woman—her face wan under her grey hair, though touched with an unreal glow from the flaming peats—in a low, crooning voice, repeated the ancient rest-words, the ancient prayer of her people, said at the covering up of the fire against the hours of sleep :—

Smalàidh mise an teine ;
Mar a smàlas Mac Moire.
Gu'm bu slàn an tigh 's an teine,
Gu'm bu slàn do'n chuideachd uile.
Co sid air an làr ?
Peadair agus Pòl,
Co air a bhith's an aire 'nochd ?
Air Moire geal 's air a Mac.
Beul De a dh' innseas,
Aingeal geal a lann'ras,
Aingeal 'an dorus gach taighe
Gu solus gael a maireach.

I will cover up the fire aright,
Even as directed by the Virgin's Son.
Safe be the house, and safe the fire,
And safe from harm be all the indwellers.
Who is that that I see on the floor ?
Even Peter himself and Paul.

50

Upon whom shall *this* night's vigil res*t*?
Upon the blameless Virgin and her Son :
God's mou*t*h has spoken it.
A whi*t*e-robed angel shall be wi*t*h us in the
    dark,
Till the coming of the sun at morn.

When she ceased, there was no sound save the low sobbing of Lora and the quiet breathing of the sleeper in the high-backed chair.

Having made the sign of the cross upon her breast and over the fire, she covered up the flame with ash and charred peat. Quietly, then, she placed her strong arm around Alastair, and half guided, half lifted him to the bed in the adjoining room where he and Lora were wont to sleep. The girl-wife followed, and, with deft hands, unclad Alastair and laid him gently in the bed. Swiftly disrobing herself, she lay down by his side, her dark hair mingling on the pillow with his tangle of dull gold.

The gleam still emitted between the bars from beneath the covered peats passed into the room through the open doorway and fell upon the bed.

Alastair stirred ; opened his eyes ; looked with wild, startled gaze at Lora, then at Mrs. Maclean, who had again knelt, and with raised arms had begun her " Blessing of Peace."

With a sigh he closed his eyes, and

the terror passed from his face. Once or twice he muttered parts of the lines of that ancient sleep-prayer, familiar to him since his boyhood, and before it was ended deep slumber had come upon him.

Laidhidh mise 'nochd
Le Moire 's le 'Mac,
Le mathair mo Righ,
'Ni mo dhion 'o dhroch-bheairt,
Cha laidh mise leis an olc,
'S cha laidh an t' olc leam ;
Ach laidhidh mì le Dia,
'S laidhidh Dia ma' rium.
Lamh dheas Dhe fo'm cheann,
Crois nan naoi aingeal leam.
'O mhullach mo chinn
Gu craican mo bhonn.
Guidheam Peadair, guidheam Pòl,
Guidheam Moir-Oigh' 'sa Mac.
Guidheam an da ostal deug,
Gun mise 'dhol eug le'n cead.
'Dhia 'sa Mhoire na gloire.
'S a Mhic na oighe cubhraidh
Cumabh mise o na piantan dorcha,
'S Micheal geal' an cò 'ail m'anama.

This night I will lay me down to sleep
With Mary Virgin and her Son,
Even with the mother of my King,
Who protects me from all evil ;
Nor shall evil lie down to sleep with me,
But I shall sleep with God :
And with me shall God lie down.
His right arm shall be under my head :
The cross of the Nine Angels be about me,
From the top of my head
To the soles of my feet.

I supplicate Peter, I supplicate Paul,
I supplicate Mary the Virgin and her Son,
I supplicate the twelve Apostles,
That evil befal us not this night.
Mary, in thy goodness and glory,
And Thou, Son of the sweet-savoured Virgin,
Protect us this night from all the pains of
    darkness.
And thou, Michael, guardian of souls, abide
    with us, watching.

When she looked down, at the end of
her prayer, Mary saw that Lora's eyes
also were closed; though by the mutter-
ing of the lips she knew her dear one
was not asleep.

Softly she closed the door behind
her; then, passing by the fire, went into
the third room of the cottage.

Soon she too was in bed, softly
repeating, as the weariness of sleep
came over her—

Cha laidh mise leis an olc,
'S cha laidh an t' olc leam.

Without, came the rising sound of
the tide among the pebbles on the
shore, the incessant chime of wave
lapsing over wave on flat rocks. The
sough of the wind fell from the corries
of Craig-an-Iolair, and died in whispers
among the fern and dew-cold grasses.

So went the hours from silence into
silence. And in time came the dawn,
and an ashen-grey upon the sea, and a

grey gloom upon each leaf and every dusky frond and blade. But when the black of the mainland became gold, and a trouble of light moved, swiftly-throbbing, across the eastern water, Michael the Watcher withdrew.

At the window of the room where Alastair and Lora slept, the beautiful sunflood of the new day poured in re-joicingly.

One long streamer of light fell upon his yellow hair and kissed the eyelids of a veiled, subsiding mind. Downward it moved, and filled with its gleam the dark-brown hair which lay across the white breast of Lora. Then, surely, it passed beneath the flower of her bosom and into her heart, and warmed it with joy ; for with a smile she awoke, murmuring, "*Pharais, Pharais.*"

[II.

EFORE the wane of that day, the rumour went among the scant population of Innisròn that Alastair, son of Diarmid of Macleod, was mad : that, in the phrasing of the islesmen, he had the mind-dark.

Men and women whispered the thing with awe. In the West, something almost of a hieratic significance is involved in the poetic phrase that God has filled with dusk the house of the brain. Not thus is spoken of the violence of insanity—the mere insurgence of delirium from the fever of hate, or from jealousy, or love, or evil of the blood, or the curse of drink. But that veil of darkness which comes down upon the mind of man or woman in the fulness of life, and puts an impermeable mist or a twilight of awful gloom about the soul, is looked upon not only with an exceeding tenderness, but with awe, and as of a bowing of the head before a divine mystery.

Yet the rumour was not true, for Alastair Macleod, though he stood within the shadow, had not yet sunk into the darkness.

As it had chanced, Mrs. Maclean was not the only person who had seen him and Lora on their return.

Late in the night Ian Maclean had come back from the western side of the isle, and was standing in the shadow of the byre when, hand in hand, Lora and Alastair approached.

The old man had been unhappy, and, after leaving his kinsman at Ardfeulan, had wandered up among the corries. In the wail of the wind along the heights, in the sough of it in the little glens and shelving uplands, he heard voices to which he would fain not have listened, for they spoke of a terror that was in the air.

The moment he saw Alastair's eyes, dark within the moonlit pallor of the face, he knew that his premonitions were no mere imaginings. On his forehead he saw the shadow of doom.

With a sigh he turned, and, having entered the byre and gone to the part of it shut off for his use, lay down upon his bed of fragrant fern.   But, weary as he was, he could not sleep.

Again the vision came to him : and once more he saw Alastair move blindly in an unfamiliar place, with the mist no longer up to his waist only, but risen now to his throat, and with thin tongues reaching upward still.

The long night went drearily past. When the day was come, Ian rose and let out the kye.   The sweet freshness of the air was as balm to his weariness. The wind blew cool upon his brows, and a breath of the sea mingled with the myriad suspiration of the earth and gave him the intoxication of the dawn.   His eyes grew brighter, his step firmer, his mien no longer that of profound dejection ; and when Ghaoth came leaping towards him, and barked about the half amused, half angry cows —who stopped to plash their hooves in the thick white dew, against which the warm breaths fell revolvingly like grey whorls of steam, and to swing their great horns against their flanks, wild and shaggy as the brown hill-sides in autumn — then all the gloom of the night went from him.

" Mayhap it was but a dream," he muttered : " and who can tell the folly of the mind ? "

Then, with Ghaoth's help, he got the

steers from the neighbouring shed and " Righ-geal," the great tawny-shaggy bull, whose either horn could have pierced right through and beyond the biggest drover who ever crossed the Kyles at Colintraive, and urged all the kine upward to the higher pastures, where the thyme was so sweet, close-clustered as it was among the soft green hair of the isle-grass.

It seemed to him as though all the larks on Innisròn were singing at one time and just there, everywhere around and above him. In the birk-shaws, there was a mavis that was as a fount where-from music spilled intoxicatingly : by the burn, the merles called, re-called, and called yet again, and over and over, sweet and blithe, and with loud, reck-less cries of mirth and joy. On every gorse-bush, yellow with bloom, fragrant almost to pain, and filled with the murmur of the wild-bee and the high, thin hum of the wood-wasp, a yellow-hammer flitted to and fro, or sang its *tweet — tweet — tweet—o-o-oh sweet !— sweet !*

The sky was almost cloudless save for an angry flush in the north-east—a deep, living blue of infinite, though in-discernibly faint gradation. Here and there, too, were thin, almost invisible grey mares' - tails swept upward, as though they were snow-dust or sea-spray, before the flying feet of the Weaver of the Winds.

As soon as Ian had reached the last dyke, and had seen " Righ-geal " lead his impatient following towards the uplands, he stood swaying his grey head slowly to and fro, with his right hand moving automatically in rhythmic ac cord, while he repeated the familiar " Rann Buachailleachd," or Rune on the driving of the cattle to the pastures :—

Siubhal beinne, siubhal coille,
Siubhal gu rèidh fada, farsuinn,
Banachag Phadruig ma'n casan,
'S gu faic mise slàn a rithisd sith.
An seun a chuir Moire mu 'buar,
Moch 'us anmoch 'sa tigh'n bhuaidh',
Ga'n gleidheadh O pholl, O eabar.
O fheithe, O adh'rcean a cheile,
O liana' na Craige-Ruaidhe,
'S o Luaths na Féinne.
Banachag Phadruig ma'r casan,
Gu'm bu slàn a thig sibh dhachaidh.

Wandering o'er uplands, wandering thro'
    woods,
Hence and far away wander ye still,
St. Patrick's own milkmaid attend your steps
Till safe I see you return to me again.
The charm that Mary made to her cattle,
Early and late, going and coming from pas-
    ture,
Still keep you safe from quagmire and marsh,
From pitfalls and from each other's horns,

*Fr*om the sudden swelling by the Red Rock,
And from the hound Lua*t*h of the Fingalians.
St. Pa*t*rick's milkmaid a*t*tend your fee*t*,
Safe and sca*t*heless come ye home again.

Then, calling Ghaoth from the already scattered kye, he turned and made his way back to the clachan.

When he entered Mrs. Maclean's cottage, where his breakfast of porridge was ready, he made and received the usual salutation of blessing : and then sat down in silence.

The room was full of sunlight—so full that Mrs. Maclean had hung a screen of bracken from an iron hook, so that it shielded the peat-fire and let the life of the flame burn unchecked.

He did not look at Alastair; and, indeed, all the morning-blitheness had gone out of the eyes of the old man. Not that any there noticed his taciturnity. Mrs. Maclean moved softly to and fro. Alastair sat broodingly in the leathern chair before the fire : Lora on a stool at his feet, with her right hand claspt in his left and her eyes fixt on his face. On the table the porridge was untouched, the new bread uncut, the warm milk grown tepid.

With a sigh, Alastair rose at last. Crossing the room, he went to the east window and stared forth unseeingly, or, at any rate, without sign of any kind.

Then, restlessly, he began to pace to and fro. Repressing her tears, Lora seated herself at the table and tried to eat, hopeful that she might thus induce him to do likewise. Mrs. Maclean followed her example, but ate in silence. She had almost ended, when Lora saw that she had abruptly laid down her spoon and was looking intently at Ian.

The old man now followed every motion of the invalid with a look as of one fascinated. When, suddenly, Alastair turned, went to the door and crossed the threshold, Ian rose and followed.

A few seconds later he came back, his withered face almost as white as his hair.

Mrs. Maclean met him ere he could speak.

"Not a word before *her*," she whispered. " Meet me at the byre: I shall be there in a minute or two."

But just then Lora rose and went out.

"Ian Maclean, what is it?"

"Mary, my kinswoman, he is not alone."

"Not alone?"

" I have seen *the other*."

She knew now what he meant. He had seen the shadow-self, the phantasm of the living that, ere death, is often seen alongside the one who shall soon die. Mrs. Maclean knew well that this shadowy second-self simulated the real self, and that even all the actions of the body were reproduced with a grotesque verisimilitude. But she was also aware how, sometimes, one may learn from the mien of the phantasm what is hidden in the aspect of the doomed.

" Last night," Ian went on in a dull voice, " I had the sight again. I saw the mist of death as high about him as when a man is sunken in a peat-bog up to the eyes."

" Well ? I know you have more to say."

" Aye."

" Speak, Ian ! "

With a long, indrawn breath, the o'd man resumed in a slow, reluctant voic .

" When I came in, a little ago, I saw the sorrow there was on every face. My vision, too, came back upon me, and I had trouble. I meant to eat and go out quickly. But when Mr. Alastair began to move about, I saw that he was not alone. I knew *the other* at once. There could be no mistake. In dress, in height, in face, in movement, they were the same. But there was a difference."

Mrs. Maclean shuddered slightly, and her lips opened as though she were about to speak. With a gesture, however, she signed to Ian to continue.

"Aye, there was a difference. I hoped against my eyes; but when I followed him yonder I saw what I saw, and what killed my hope."

"Speak, speak, Ian!"

"In all things the same but one, and that was in the eyes, in the expression. Those of Mr. Alastair were dull and lightless, and brooding low; those of *the other* were large and wild, and stared in terror and amaze; and on the face of the thing the Fear lay, and moved, and was alive."

"O Ian, Ian, what does it mean?"

"It means this, Mary, daughter of Donnacha, what, sure, you know well: that not only is the shadow of death near this house, but that upon Alastair Mac Diarmid is the mind-dark that lay upon his father and upon his father's father."

"The curse of Michael be upon this evil, Ian!"

"Even so, *Mhoire nighean Donnacha.*"

"His father was the third of his race in succession who, soon or late, fell under that shadow. And we all know, sure we all know, that after the third generation the veil is withdrawn. This

thing is an evil dream of yours, Ian
Maclean!"

"It is an evil doing of *some one*,"
muttered the old man, with sombre
eyes.

"Perhaps"— . . .

But before Mrs. Maclean could say
what was in her mind, Alastair and
Lora entered.

With downcast eyes Ian passed out,
giving a furtive, terrified look behind
him ere he closed the door.

It was through the old isleman that
the rumour of Alastair Macleod's mad-
ness went abroad.

Long before the stormy afternoon
which followed the beautiful youth of
that day, with its ominous morning-red
in the north-east, had waned to gloam-
ing, there was not a soul on Innisròn
who did not know of the sorrow.

Yet no one came near out of a cruel
sympathy: no one spoke heedless words
either of question or solace to Mrs.
Maclean; for none could be said to
the two most concerned, neither
Alastair nor Lora having been seen
throughout the day.

Nevertheless, a deep resentment
prevailed against one person upon the
island. Not only had the Spring gone
ill with the fishing, but the nets had

been torn and trailed in a way that suggested something beyond the blind malice of wind and wave and the currents of the deep sea and the savage dog-fish. Several cows had ceased to give milk; hens had ceased to lay; and Gregor McGregor's white mare had dropped a dead foal, the first time such a thing had happened on the isle. And now that, unforeseen and in the heyday of youth and health, the worst of all troubles had come upon Alastair Macleod, many recalled how his father, Macleod of Dunvrechan, who had died on Innisròn, had not only once denounced old Ealasaid MacAodh as a woman of the evil eye, but had cursed her ere he died, and attributed his misery to a blight of her working.

As one spake to another, the same thought came into each mind : that the old widow who lived at Craig-Ruaidh, at the head of the Glen of the Dark Water, had put her malice upon Alastair Mac Diarmid.

Some one, in a group by the ferry, reminded her hearers that, by a mis-chance, every one on the isle save Widow MacAodh had been invited to the feast in the little mission-house, when "*Lora nighean maighstir Tor-maid*" was wedded : and how it was well known that old Ealasaid had been full of anger and pain at the slight, and had since scarce spoken with any one save Mrs. Maclean, with whom no bitterness was ever long to endure.

" Ay, ay, it's her doing — it's her doing," was muttered all round; " she has put the spell of the evil eye upon him—foreigner that she is."

Many years had gone by since Duncan bàn MacAodh, a Hebridean who had settled in Innisròn, brought thither a wife out of remote St. Kilda. Long since he had gone to his rest, and lay among the few dead under the great runic cross at the extreme of Ardfeulan, on the west of the isle: yet he was still " the man from Uist," as his widow was still the " outlander."

" Ian," said Pòl Macdonald, one of the oldest of the fishermen, " you too are said to have *the thing* in you, though you always look through both eyes, and with good will to man and beast. Let you, and two others of us, go to-night to Widow Ealasaid's, and do you look upon her and find out if she is accursed: . . . and then . . . and then . . ."

No one spoke, though a veiled consenting glance went between Macdonald and Ian and a young islesman, Ronald Macrae, who lived over by Ardfeulan.

It was not a subject to discuss further in that hour of uncertainty. One o two members of the group had already edged away, when Kathia Macdonald suddenly drew attention to the appearance of the first three of the returning herring-boats, anxiously expected for over an hour past.

The brown-sailed wherries came in under the lee of the isle in a smother of foam. Already a snarling north-easter was racing over the sea, still smelling of the ling and bracken it had flattened as it tore over the summits of the mainland hills.

The water was of a shifting emerald near the haven ; of a dark bottle-green beyond ; and, out in the open, black, fretted and torn with staring white splashes and a myriad-leaping surge.

The race of the sea-horses had begun, and no one on Innisròn was at ease till the last boat had come safely round from Ardgheal, the point whence on the yestereve Lora had so eagerly watched for the coming of her husband.

A fiery sunset disclosed the immense and swirling procession of clouds high over the isle —cloud not only racing after cloud, but often leaping one upon the other as flying sheep in panic. Towards the east, the vapours were larger and darker : the cohorts more densely massed. Above the mainland stretched one vast unbroken phalanx of purple-livid gloom, out of the incessant and spasmodically convulsive travail in whose depths swept monstrous cloud-births.

As the night fell, there was audible beyond the hills the noise of a baffled thunderstorm—a tempest which had been caught among the mountains, and could no more lift itself over the summits than a screaming and wrestling eagle could tear itself from a stag in whose hide its talons had become irremovably gript.

Above the peaks and along the flank of the mass of livid gloom, spears of lightning were swung against the wind ; and with splinter and flash, there was a rain of whirled lances as against some unseen assault from below.

The tumult soared, hurled downward, and fell upon Innisròn. The islefolk listened in the dark with awe. Roar and crash, and a frightful, terrifying howling followed every blast, as of a volcano belching forth avalanche after avalanche, and shaking to the valleys the *débris* of all the hills. Roar upon roar, crash upon crash, howl upon howl: with the strident raucous scream of the wind, yelling a pæan of triumph as it leapt before the javelins of the lightning and tore in its ruinous might far out across the heaving, swaying, moaning sea.

It was a night for all who fare by or upon the deep waters to remember with awe : for those whose lives, and kin, and gear had gone scatheless, to recollect with thanksgiving : for those whose weal went with it, to recall with bowed heads or wet eyes.

An hour or more after nightfall, three figures moved with the wind across the isle : blurred shadows astir in the tempest-riven dark. Ronald Macrae carried a lantern ; but speedily laid it down by a cairn, for the flame could not live.

He and Ian and Pòl were grimly silent, not only on the path through the wind-swept heather, but when under shelter from a bight of hillside or over-hanging crag. The business that took them out in that tempest lay heavy upon them.

If, out of her own mouth, or by sign or deed of her own, Ealasaid should convict herself of the use of the evil-eye, her doom would be fixt. Even in the bitterness of superstition, however, the islemen were not bent upon the extreme penalty, the meed of those who deal in witchcraft. The dwellers on Innisròn, as all who live among the outer isles in general, are too near the loneliness of life and death to be wanton in the taking away of that which is so great in the eyes of man and so small in the eyes of God.

The worst they intended was to make Ealasaid bring her own doom upon her: then, on the morrow, her sheiling would be burned to the ground and the ashes scattered to the four quarters, while she herself would be exiled from the island under ban of cross, mystic word, and the ancient Celtic anathema.

So wild was the wind and dark the way, that a full hour passed before they reached the Glen of the Dark Water, and heard the savage ramping and charging of the endless squadrons of the waves against the promontory of Ardfeulan.

As they drew near the little cottage, a lonely dwelling on the brae which sloped to the glen, they saw that the occupant had not yet gone to bed, for a red gleam of light stole comfortingly across the forlorn dark.

With a significant touch on the shoulder of each of his companions, Ian led them to within a yard or two of the window.

"Hush," he whispered, in a momentary lull; "make no noise as we look in. She might hear, and blast us with her evil eye. Perhaps she is even now talking with some warlock or fiend."

Trembling, the three men huddled under the wall. At last, slowly, and with hearts wildly athrob, they raised themselves and looked within.

The room was bare in its clean poverty. On the rickety wooden table was a bowl with a little unfinished porridge in it. A yard away was an open Gaelic Bible, with a pair of horn spectacles laid across the open page. At a spinning stool between the table and the peat-fire was an old woman, kneeling, with her hands claspt and her face upraised. On the poor, tired, worn features was a look of pathetic yearning, straining from a white and beautiful peace.

So rapt was she that she did not see a hand move the outer latch of the window, or feel the sudden breath of the night-air.

Then those without, waiting to hearken to sorcery more appalling than the savagery of the tempest, heard old Ealasaid repeat this prayer:

Tha 'n la nis air falbh ùainn,
Tha 'n oidhche 'tighinn orm dlùth ;
'S ni mise luidhe gu dion
Fo dhubhar sgiath mo rùin.

O gach cunnart 's o gach bàs,
'S o gach nàmhaid th' aig Mac Dhe,
O nàdur dhaoine borba,
'S o choirbteachd mo nàduir fèin,
Gabhaidh mis' a nis armachd Dhe,
Gun bhi reubta no brisd',
'Sge b' oil leis an t'sàtan 's le phàirt
Bi'dh mis' air mo gheàrd a nis.

The day is now gone ;
Dark night gathers around,
And I will lay me safely down (to sleep)
Under the shadow of my Beloved One's wing.
Against all dangers, and death in every form,
Against each enemy of God's good Son,
Against the anger of the turbulent people,
And against the corruption of my own nature,
I will take unto me the armour of God—
That shall protect me from all assaults :
And in spite of Satan and all his following,
I shall be well and surely guarded.

When, after an interval of speechless prayer, the lonely old woman rose painfully to her feet, she noticed the open window, and heard the sough of the wind without.

With a tired sigh, she crossed the room to close the inside latch. But, at the window, she stood irresolute, held by the noise of the sea beating against the clamour of the wind. She stooped, and peered forth.

Not a thing was visible. Suddenly a broad wavering gleam of sheet-lightning lit up the whole brae. Almost, she fancied, she could have sworn she saw three human figures, with bowed heads, moving across the brow of the slope.

She could not know that three men, stricken with shame and remorse— remorse which would ere long bloom into the white flower of repentance, to be worn lovingly by all on the isle— were stealing homeward from a vain and wicked errand.

With a shudder, she crossed herself, fearing that the figures she had imagined, or had really seen, were the three dreadful Accursed who drove the spear into Christ's side and the nails into His hands and feet, and with mocking offered Him the bitter sponge.

Slowly repeating—

O gach cunnart 's o gach bàs,
'S o gach nàmhaid th' aig Mac Dhe,

she quenched with charred peat the flame of her fire, and was soon in a child-like rest " under the shadow of the wing of her Beloved One."

When midnight came upon the isle, the worst violence of the storm was over. Nevertheless, upon the sea was the awfulness of desolation, the rumour of a terrible wrath.

All slept at last : the innocent Ealasaid, the foolish seekers of evil, the islefolk one and all—except two.

Alastair and Lora lay in each other's arms as children terrified in the dark.

That afternoon his madness had come upon him for a while; and he had smiled grimly at he knew not what, and laughed while the tears streamed from the eyes of Lora and Mary; and moaned betimes; and cried out against the calling of the sea; and closed his ears against the frightful wailing of a kelpie in the tarn beyond the byre; and, at the last, shook as in an ague before the fire, fearful of some informulate terror, but with such a crown of sorrow on his forehead that the two women bowed their faces in their hands, speechless with grief: with such a horror in his eyes that Ghaoth shrank from him with bristling fell and upcurled, snarling lip.

But with the night came yet another merciful lifting of the veil.

While the storm raged at its worst, the three kneeled, and Mrs. Maclean read from the beautiful Gaelic Scripture. Then, with all the tenderness of her childless passion of maternity, she prayed for God's balm and peace and the healing of His hand.

When, in time, she went to her own

room, Alastair and Lora talked for long in a low voice.

On the day he had first heard that the seed of life had taken root in her womb, and knew that a child was to be born of their great love, he had known a thrill of such rapture that he could scarce see Lora for the blinding of the tears of joy.

Beautiful she was to all : to him, lovely and tender as twilight and dear beyond words : but at that moment, when he learned from her own lips of her only half explicable trouble, he knew he had passed into a Holy of Holies of love and reverent passion such as he had but vaguely dreamed of as possible.

But now, on this wild night of storm without and more awful dread within, he recalled with horror what had been driven from his mind.

Bitter as was the doom he and Lora had to face, tenfold bitter was it made by the thought that they were to bring into the world yet another soul shrouded in the shadow of his own intolerable ill.

And so it was that, at the last, Alastair and Lora Macleod, knowing his madness was at hand and could be cured of no man, and that their lives were spilled out as lees from a cup, and that they were witlessly dooming the unborn child to a heritage of grief, gave solemn troth to each other that on the morrow they would go forth hand in hand, and, together in death as in life, lay themselves beneath that ever wandering yet ever returning wave which beats day and night, and week by week, and year by year, and without end for ever, about the sea-gathered graveyard on the remote west of Innisròn.

Then was a great peace theirs. For the last time they laid themselves down on their bed : for the last time twined their arms around each other, while on the same pillow their heads lay side by side, the hair about his forehead wet with her falling tears : for the last time they kept vigil through the terror of the dark—an awful terror now, with the wrath of the sea without, with the shadow of Death within the room, with the blackness of oblivion creeping, creeping from chamber to chamber in the darkened house of a dulled, subsiding brain.

Ere dawn, Alastair slept. Lora lay awake, trembling, longing for the day, yet praying God to withhold it; sick with baffled hope, with the ache of weariness, with the sound of the moan and hollow boom of the sea. More

deep and terrible in her ears grew that
midnight Voice, reverberant in the
room as in the whorl of a shell: a
dreadful iterance of menace, a dirge
that confusedly she seemed to know
well, a swelling chant, a requiem.

IV.

AN hour after sunrise there was not
a cloud in the sky. The first
day of June came clad in the fulness
of summer. Sea and land seemed as
though they had been immersed in
that Fount of Life which wells from
the hollow of the Hand which up-
holdeth Tir-na-h'Oighe, the isle of
eternal youth.

The low island-trees had not suf-
fered as had those on the mainland :
yet everywhere were strewn branches,
and, on the uplands, boughs wrenched
away, and often hurled far from the
parent tree.

But upon all the isle there was now a
deep quiescence. In the warm languor,
even the birds sang less wildly clear,
though the high, remote, falling lark-
music floated spirally earthward, poig-

nantly sweet. An indescribably delicate
shimmer of haze lay on the heights
and pastures, and where the corries
sloped jaggedly seaward, each with a
singing burn splashing or wimpling
adown its heart. From the uplands
came the lowing of the kine, the bleat-
ing of the ewes and lambs, the rapid
whirring gurgle of the grouse among
the heather. The wailing of curlews
rose and fell ; the sharp cries of the
cliff-hawks beat against Craig-Ruaidh.
High overhead, as motionlessly in
motion as the snow-white disc of the
moon lying immeasurably more remote
within the vast blue hollow of the sky,
an eagle poised on outspread wings,
and then, without visible effort or move-
ment, drifted slowly out of sight like a
cloud blown by the wind.

Only upon the sea was something of
the tumult of the past night still a
reality.

Around the isle, and in the wide
Sound between it and the mainland,
the " white sheep " moved in endless
procession, no longer wildly dispersed
and huddled and torn by the wolves of
the tempest. Oceanward the sea-horses
swept onward magnificently, champing
and whirling white foam about their
green flanks, and tossing on high their
manes of sunlit rainbow gold, dazzling-

white and multitudinous far as sight could reach.

Clamour of gulls, noise of waves, lisp and chime and flute-call of the shallows among the rock-holes and upon the whispering tongues of the sea-weed— what joy, and stir, and breath of life!

Hand in hand, in the hot noon, Lora and Alastair went idly along the sheep-path leading from the clachan to the promontory of Ardgheal. The smell of the brine from the sea and wrack-strewn shore, the sun-wrought fragrance of the grass and thyme, of bracken and gale, of birch and hawthorn and trail-ing briar, of the whole beautiful, living, warm body of the earth so lay upon the tired senses with a healing as of balm, that even the tears in Lora's eyes ceased to gather, leaving there only a softness as of twilight-dew in violets.

It was to be their last walk in the sunshine of that day—their last par-ticipance in the sunshine of life.

All the morning had been spent by Alastair in writing and brooding. Once again he had talked over with Lora that projected deed, which to them seemed the one right and fitting end to the tragedy of circumstance. She had promised that even if the darkness came down upon his mind irretrievably she would fulfil her troth with him.

Great love casteth out fear; but even if this had not been so with her, she bore in mind the menace of what he had said about the child.

She, too, had spent a little of that last morning in writing, though her letter was not to go across the sea to the mainland, but to be left with old Ian to give to Mary on the morrow.

It was close upon noon when she saw that Alastair's gloom was upon him again, though he was now as quiet as a child. Taking his hand, she led him forth, heedful to avoid the clachan, and vaguely wishful to visit once more that little eastern haven of Ardgheal where, but two days ago, she had longingly awaited Alastair's return, and where, months before, he had first won her love.

He seemed to take pleasure in the sight of the sea he loved so well, and in the songs of the birds, and to be vaguely displeased because Ghaoth would not leap to his caress as usual, or else would crouch at his feet with startled eyes and low whine.

When Lora spoke, he answered seldom; but when he did, she knew that he understood. Once or twice he looked at her strangely; and once, with a thrill of awe and dread, she saw that it was unrecognisingly.

With a sob, she turned and put her arms about him. Never had he seemed so fair in her sight—tall and comely as a young pine, of a beauty beyond that of any man she had ever seen. No wonder that her father, familiar lover of the Ossianic ballads, had been wont, remembering the beauty of the second son of Usnoth, lord of Etha, to call Alastair *Ailthos*.

"Dear, my dear one, Ailthos, Alastair!" she cried, clinging close. "Look at me! Speak to me! Do you not know me?"

Slowly he turned his eyes upon her, and after a brief perplexity the shadow went out of them, and he smiled gently.

"Let us go home, my fawn," he whispered. "I am tired. It would be too sad to go down to Ardgheal."

He had already caught sight of the smoke of a steamer beyond Dunmore Point; and fearing that it might be the *Clansman*—for he thought the hour much later than it was—he hoped to spare Lora another needless pang. Moreover, his growing dread of seeing any one was stronger than ever upon him.

So they turned thus soon even in that last sunshine, and, entering the cottage, sat before the smouldering peat-fire; he brooding darkly, Lora dreaming through her slow-welling tears, and both . . . . waiting.

Though, at dusk, a heavy sea still ran, it was partly due to the surge of the ground-swell and to the turbulence of the tide, for there was but little wind even away from the shelter of the isle, and what there was came mostly in short, sudden puffs and wandering breaths.

In the quietude of the gloaming, it was as though the sea called all round Innisròn as a beast of prey stalks about a high sheepfold, growling, breathing heavily, ravening.

After the supper, eaten frugally and in silence, Lora and Alastair listened once again to the peat-prayer and the Blessing of Peace of Mrs. Maclean ; then, not daring to say any word to her but that of a husky farewell for the night, and fearful even of meeting the glance of her quiet eyes, they went to their room, there to sit silently awhile in the darkness, hand in hand.

No one saw them leave the cottage an hour later : not a soul heard them as they passed through the clachan.

The road they chose was that sheep-path through the heather which led to Ardfeulan by the Glen of the Dark Water. Each knew the way well, otherwise their faring westward would have been difficult, for the sky was veiled by a thin mist and the moon was not visible.

They walked in silence ; sometimes Lora in advance, but, whenever practicable, together, and hand in hand.

At last they reached the Glen of the Dark Water, and perceived through the gloaming the sheiling of Ealasaid MacAodh. This they skirted, and then entered a sloping hollow, at the base of which was audible the hoarse murmuring of the sea. Lora knew the place well. A week ago she had been there with Alastair, and remembered that the whole slope was a mass of moonflowers, tall, white, and so close-clustered that the green stems could hardly be seen.*

The wan glimmer of them was perceptible now, like the milky way on a night when a faint frost-mist prevails. Around, there was nothing else visible. Not a tree grew in that place : not a crag rose out of the sea of death-white blooms. The low-hanging mist-cloud veiled all things. It was as though the grave had been passed, and this was the gloom of the Deathsleep Land that lies beyond. Only *there* is eternal

---

* A tall, cream-white marguérite, native to the Outer Isles and the Hebrides, is known to the Islanders as the Moonflower.

silence : here, the dull menace of the sea made a ceaseless murmur about the obscure coasts.

As they entered the valley of moon-flowers, dimly seeing their way a few yards beyond them, and hearkening to the inwash and resurgence of the tide moving along the extreme frontiers of the land, a sense of unspeakable dread came over Alastair and Lora.

They stood still, hardly daring to breathe. Both vaguely remembered something : they knew not what, save that the tragic memory was linked with reminiscence of a valley of moonflowers seen in a dark twilight. Was it all a dream, coincident in their minds ? Or had life once before, in some unre-membered state, wrought tragic issues for them by a valley of white flowers seen in the darkness, with a deeper darkness around, a veiled sky above, and the hoarse, confused prophesying of the sea beyond ?

As they stood, the moon—about an hour risen—glimmered through the veil of cloud. As with a hand, the rift was slowly made ; but though the light was now clearly visible, it still gleamed through filmy shrouds of vapour. There was no shape, no central luminous spot even : only a diffused sheen which spread for a great span northward and southward, though it illumed nothing beneath save the long sloping hollow filled with moonflowers. The blooms rose almost to the knees of the two silent and trembling figures. For some inscrutable reason, the advance of light had not brought any comfort to either : rather, their vague terror increased almost unendurably.

The sea called below. Lora shuddered, and drew back a step or two.

A long, wavering, greenish light appeared high above the south-west. As the sheet-lightning fled shudderingly northward, it lapsed into ashen tremors before it was swallowed up of the darkness, as a wounded sea-bird in the deep.

In that brief gleam, Alastair turned and looked into Lora's eyes.

She moved to his side again, and once more took his hand. Then, slowly, and still without word one to the other, they moved downward through the hollow.

There was not a sound about them save the susurrus of their feet going through the moonflowers. From the glen alone came any break in the inland stillness, the noise of water running swiftly from ledge to ledge. In the darkness where the sea was, there broke the fluctuating moan and boom of ocean. From far across the wave came a thin, forlorn sound that was the crying of the wind.

Minute by minute, as they waded through that death-white wilderness, the moon wove the cloud-shroud into thinner veils, till at last, as the two figures emerged upon the shore by the side of a precipitous scaur, they were of a filmy gossamer that no longer obscured the golden-yellow globe that wheeled solemnly through the appalling upper solitudes of the night.

The tide, at the last reach of the ebb for nearly an hour past, was now on the flood : though the first indeterminate babble of returning waters was scarce different from the lapsing ebb-music in aught save a gurgling swiftly-repetitive undertone.

The scaur by whose side they stood was hollow, and was known as the Cave of the Sea-Woman. It could be reached dry-shod, or nearly so, only at low water, and even then only during calm, or when the wind did not blow from the south or west. For years beyond record it had been almost unvisited, for the cavern was a place of deadly peril except just before and after the extreme ebb. But after the death of two of his sons—one in the effort to swim outward against the inrush of the tide ; the other by falling, or being swept backward to the deep chasm that lay at the far end of the cave—old Macrae, of Ardfeulan Farm near by, had caused rude steps to be cut in the funnel-like hollow rising sheer up from the sloping ledge that lipped the chasm and reached the summit of the scaur.

The smell of the brine from the dripping boulders smote shrewdly upon Alastair and Lora as they stood at the weedy mouth of the cavern. Then for the first time that night they turned their backs upon the sea, and moved slowly across the long, flat slabs of rock.

It was not dark at the entrance to the Cavern of the Sea-Woman, for the moonlight moved within it as the hand of a blind man groping blankly in an unfamiliar place. The arch of the rock was clear, and even the frondage of fern and sea-plants suspended from its lower curve; also, beneath, a mass of mossed crag, just beyond the highest reach of the tides. Among this dark crag-vegetation grew strange plants; but none stranger or so rare as the sea-grape, or mermaid's-fruit of the islanders. No one on Innisròn knew its proper designation, and it had become known at all as the sea-grape only because some student of rare things discovered and

wrote about it under that name, as per-
haps the culminating treasure-trove of
the botanist in the Scottish West. It
is a plant which clings as a tendril,
choosing only the summit of high
rocks or boulders in some sunless place
where it can breathe the ooze from
dead or dying seaweed, and can feel
the salt air reach it with a chilly touch.
It lies low, with its thin, moist, ash-
grey stems ; its round, pale-green, trans-
parent leaves faintly spotted with livid
blotches ; and its infrequent clusters
of small, juicy berries of a hue of dusky
yellow.

The islefolk regard it with awe.
Though the fruit is poisonous, and a
deadly draught can be distilled from
the leaves, a few berries would not suf-
fice to kill. To eat sparingly of the
sea-grape is not to invite death neces-
sarily, but to bring about a stupor
so deep that for an hour or more no
familiar sound can reach the ear, no
ordinary shock vibrate along the nerves,
no common pain affect the body. If
the eater of the mermaid's-fruit be left
undisturbed, he will not stir for twelve
or even fifteen hours, though the first
death-like trance does not prevail be-
yond an hour, or at most two: while, if
forcibly aroused, he is so weak in body
and so dazed in mind that he cannot

long be kept awake without peril to the brain, and indeed to life itself.

It was because of this fruit of oblivion that Alastair and Lora had sought the Cave of the Sea-Woman.

They had feared not so much their own instinctive evasion of death as that, in the final struggle, they might not go down into the shadow together.

The idea that the Silence should come upon them unawares—that, arms about each other in a last embrace, the wave should encroach upon their deep unheeding slumber—had given them a strange elation. The thought was Alastair's. Though he was not a native of Innisròn, he had often visited it from Dunvrechan even before he had come to love Lora, and was familiar with each of the treacherous caves and all the desolate, boulder-strewn, uninhabited south-western side of the island, as well as with everything in animate or inanimate nature which was to be found therein. Not only had he often heard of the sea-grape which grew almost inaccessibly in some of the caverns on the western side, but he knew where in the Cave of the Sea-Woman it was to be obtained with little difficulty.

Letting Lora's hand drop gently to her side, he climbed the rough, broken ledges to the right, and swiftly returned holding in his hand a cluster of limp leaves from which hung snakily several stems of the dusky-yellow fruit.

Lora looked at the berries curiously, and yet with a strange indifference. With that awful menacing sound of the sea beyond, with that more awful murmur of dread in her heart, with that rising tide of death all about them, it mattered little to her that Alastair laid such stress on those small, poisonous things, those petty messengers of a mere oblivion of the senses.

Just beyond where they stood, and at the beginning of those long, flat, inward sloping ledges which formed the floor of the cavern till the abrupt ending over the dark chasm at the extreme end, was a bed of soft white sand, shelving from one of the ledges past and underneath another, and then among rocks covered with bladder-wrack and adder's‑tongues and other sea-weed, with tangled masses of the long, trailing dead-man's-hair.

Still without speech, here Alastair and Lora lay down, side by side.

There is an ebb in the tide of human hope that must reach a limit. When this limit is attained there is too great weariness for any further revolt, for any protest, for anything but dull acquiescence.

Slowly Alastair stripped a few of the dusky berries from the plant and held them in the hollow of his hand to Lora.

Taking them, she leaned forward, looking intently upon his face, but failing to see into his eyes, because of a deeper shadow therein than that which environed them.

"*Alastair,*" she whispered.

He made no answer; but wearily raised his hand to his mouth, and with his tongue crushed against his palate the acrid juice of the sea-grapes.

"O Alastair! speak to me! speak to me!"

He turned slowly. Then suddenly he put out his arms, and gathered her to his breast.

"My beautiful gloom—Lora—my Rest—my Joy—O you who are my Pharais—all the Pharais I care for now or dream of—if there be indeed a pitiful God, He will have mercy upon us. If we do wrong, we sin believing that we are doing the right, the sole right thing. But sweet it is—O Lora, sweet and dear at the last, after all our dark bewildered pain, to be here and know that all is over now, and that we two go into the Silence together: and if there be any waking, that together we shall wake. *Mo ghràidh, mo mùir-*

nean, my dear one, what peace there is for you and me that I die thus: free from that crushing, crushing pain and darkness that has filled my brain."

"Alastair! O my dear love—dearest — shall we — shall we meet again after this dreadful night? Shall there be any day for us? I cannot die—oh, I cannot die in this awful darkness . . . thus . . . We are both so young . . . and I . . .

She ceased abruptly.

A low splashing sound, with long-drawn suffocating surge and susurrus, told that the sea had begun to creep forward with stealthy swiftness.

It was not the menace of the tide, however, that froze the words upon her lips.

Alastair had begun to croon, in a drowsy, yet strained, uncertain voice, a snatch of fisher-lore.

"Alastair! Alastair! Alastair!"

He gave a low laugh, as he turned on his side, and with wandering fingers played idly with the sand.

"Alastair! . . . my husband! . . Beloved . . . Alastair! . . . Oh, say farewell to me at the least. . . Do not turn from me!"

"It called—called—called: and she cried to me, Come, my Belovèd: and then I knew Lora was dead. Why do you laugh at me? She is dead, I tell you: *dead, dead, dead!* She, my beautiful Lora—my dream—my joy—she who to me was Pharais itself: she is *dead!*"

In the grip of supreme woe, a woman has a heroism of abnegation beyond all words to tell of it.

Her grief rose within Lora as a phantom, and chilled her to the very heart and to the very brain. But with a great effort she stirred, leaned over and pluckt some of the fatal fruit, and swallowed it: for she had crushed in her hand the berries he had given her.

Then, having risen, with deft hands she pulled towards her some long strings of dead-man's-hair and rope-weed; and, with those which were firmly affixed to rocks or heavy stones, she wove a girdle about the waist of Alastair, and so round her own.

She could scarce see to finish her task, for the moon had passed upward into the denser cloud, and the faintly luminous veils of vapour beneath it were now scarce distinguishable from the obscurity all around.

The insistent wash of the tide was coming steadily nearer. She could feel the cold breath of its moving lip.

Absolute darkness prevailed; while, with shaking hands, having unloosed her long, black hair, she tied it firmly in two places with the curly tangle of him whom she loved so passing well in death as in life.

Not a gleam fell from the veiled moon. Not a thing was visible save a faint phosphorescent line that moved slowly inward. Lora could not see Alastair's face, not even his body, not even the two shaking hands she held over him while she prayed inaudibly, and with a suffocating, bewildering pain at her heart, at her lungs, in her head.

No sound came from the isle. The noise of the falling stream in the glen was merged in the confused clamour of the tide-race. Shoreward, there was that awful tidal whisper. Seaward, the march of wave after wave, of billow after billow, in vast processional array ; squadron after squadron, battalion after battalion, of the innumerable army of the deep : and among them all, over them all, beneath them all, a Voice, loud, reverberant, menacing, awful as brooding thunder, terrible as the quaking of the dry land when the hills o'ertopple the cities of the plain : a Voice as of the majesty of Death, swelling through the night with all the eternal pain, the forlorn travail, the incommunicable ache of all the weary, weary World.

Then, ere all remembrance died for her, Lora knew that Alastair slept and was at peace.

She stole her arm round his neck and held him close, but was too weak now to lean over and kiss those white lips, parted as a child's in dreamless slumber.

It was her last pain : the last unavailing bitterness of woman's woe.

Thereafter she lay still, vaguely hearkening the tide run up the deep channel beyond the little isle of sand, already damp with the under-ooze.

She listened to the slipping of the water along the ledges. A wave came out of the darkness and stalked through the gloom as a wild beast to its lair. Ledge over ledge she heard it swiftly move : then suddenly there was a blank . . . a hoarse muffled noise . . . the hollow reverberation of the billow as it fell heavily into the black unfathomed gulf wherein at the flood was swept all that drifted into the cave.

A windy sigh arose in the cavern. The tide moved upward, feeling along the walls with stealthy, groping hands. A faint phosphorescence appeared momently, now here, now there.

The second channel, to the left, suddenly brimmed. The water spilled over upon the sandy tract beyond. Then a long rolling wave raced inward, leapt along one of its ledges, poised a moment, and, breaking into a seething foam in its fall, tore this way and that the weedy bonds which bound the sleepers.

Beyond, in the darkness, the loud moan, the deep, monotonous boom of the sea filled the whole vast void of the night.

V.

*C*HE loud and terrifying violence of
the sea throughout that day; the
oppressive gloom of that night; the
weight of undischarged electricity which
everywhere brooded; all made sleep
impossible for Ealasaid MacAodh.

So ill was she when evening set in,
that she had moved her things from
the bed in the second of the two rooms
of which the sheiling consisted, so as
to sleep in the box-bed in the larger,
within sight and feel of the fire-glow.

She had not slept there since her
husband died. Perhaps this was be-
cause that, even after the lapse of years,
she could not endure the solitudes of
memory. They had been lovers in
their youth, she and her Hebridean:
they had been lovers during their brief
married life, ere he, after the too fre-

quent wont of the islesmen, found death in the wave wherein he sought the means of life : and when his drifted body had been recovered, and laid in the island soil, she had remained his lover still. Doubtless, she thought of him even yet with his yellow hair and laughing eyes; perhaps of herself, too, as lithe of limb and with soft, fair skin as unwrinkled and hair as brown and supple as when he had first caused the trouble of a new and strange tide in the calm waters of her girl's heart.

To sleep in the bed where she had lain by his side, where a child had been born to her and had died just as with glad pain she had recognised in the little one the eyes of its father, may have seemed to her a cross of suffering which she was unable to take up and bear.

Or, it may be, there lurked darkly in her mind the ancient secret Celtic dread of sleeping in the bed where any of one's own blood-kin has died : the dread of the whisper that is on the pillow in the dark hours, of the hand that gropes along the coverlet, of the chill breath that comes without cause and stirs the hair as it falls suddenly upon the cheek of the awakened sleeper.

On this night, however, she dreaded not only her own weakness, but the dark. Vaguely, she wondered how she had for so long a time slept away from the comforting light and warmth of her peat-fire.

She was so old, so weary, she thought pitifully. Would Duncan be sure to know her again? Why was she kept so long there, waiting for the summons that never came? Had God forgotten her? No kin had she: not one to claim her body for the place of sleep when her dark hour came. Useless were her days to all: to herself, each day a rising sorrow; each night a setting grief.

Yet that infinite patience of the poor was hers, that poignant pathos of womanhood in childless and husband-less old age, which to the very end endures—till the last thread has been used in the weaving of the Crown of Sorrow.

Beautiful this austere Diadem worn by aged and lonely women: sweet-eyed bearers of crowns among the myriad procession of the weary poor of all the world, all going gloriously apparelled and wreathed with green garlands which fade not in the sight of Him who leadeth His feeble folk to kingship and honour.

For a brief while she lay brooding, with dull old eyes fixt upon the red heart of the peats. Then the gaze withdrew slowly, and the lids closed ; as though a bird, flying softly through the twilight, had passed beneath the low-hung leaves over its nest.

She could not have been long asleep, for the glow was still ruddy upon the floor, when she was startled by a sudden barking and whining. She sat up, listening intently. She could hear no step, no voice. The whining terrified her. If the noise were that of a dog at all, and not of Luath or some other phantom hound, whose dog was it, and why its sudden appearance at her door at that hour of night,—its eager, unceasing clamour ?

But when, with louder and louder barks and an impatient scraping, the unwelcome visitor showed he was not to be denied, she rose, put on her things, and then, having wrapt a shawl about her head and lit a lantern which she lifted from a hook, opened the door.

For a moment, she thought that nothing was there. Then her ears caught the sound of panting breath, and something wet and warm touched her suspended left hand.

With timid, yet caressing voice, she lured the dog across the threshold.

The moment she could see clearly, she recognised him as Ghaoth, the white-breasted, tawny-haired, amber-eyed collie that belonged to Alastair Mac-leod.

The dog would not bide. His whining never ceased, save when it was interrupted by loud, eager barks. To and fro he ran, and at last sprang out into the night again, only to return a few moments later in a state of excitement bordering on frenzy.

"Some evil must have happened to Alastair Macleod," Ealasaid muttered, as after a brief hesitation she took the lantern and followed Ghaoth.

To her dismay, the dog tried to lead her towards the hollow of the moon-flowers. Could Alastair possibly be there, or on the shore beyond? Why, if he were down there, lying helpless, the tide would be upon him shortly, and then his doom would be certain. Again, of what avail was she, so old and frail, and now with some new weakness upon her? She feared she had not the strength to move downward in the dark through that dense jungle of white blooms : still less to climb home-ward again.

But while she pondered, she saw that Ghaoth leapt no more in the direction of the valley, but along the grassy ridge which led to the summit of Craig-Geal, so perilous by night because of the sloping, precipitous hole which gave entrance to the funnel-like passage issuing from the Cave of the Sea-Woman.

"Ah," she cried, as it flashed upon her that Alastair had fallen, or been hemmed-in in the cavern by the tide, "God help him if he is *there !*"

With panting breath she hurried along the ridge, heedless now of Ghaoth, who had suddenly darted off to the left and disappeared among the moonflowers. She had not gone far, however, before she stopped. What use to hurry onward, if all she could do was to shout down into the darkness—a cry that would likely never be heard, and if heard would be of no avail to the hearer?

No sooner did she realise the uselessness of her errand than she turned, and, with shaking limbs and labouring breath, made her way along a sheep-path which led to the opposite brae of Craig - Ruaidh, where Angus Macrae and his son Ranald lived.

So exhausted was the old woman by the time she had reached the farm and aroused the inmates, that two or three minutes passed before she could explain.

Ranald Macrae saw at once that one of two things had happened : either that Alastair had wandered to the cave in his madness, and there, ignorant or oblivious of the steps cut in the hollow columnar passage at the far end, been cut off by the sea ; or else that he had wittingly made his way there, with intent to drown himself in the Kelpie's Pool—an abyss that never gave back what it swallowed.

It was during this hurried explana-nation to his father that Ealasaid learned for the first time the truth of what had reached her as a vague rumour in the mouth of a herd-boy. Eager as she was to be of help, she was now too weak to accompany the men, even if it were possible for her to keep pace with them, which it was not, as they had started off at a run.

She knew that old Macrae's advice was right : that she could best help by going home at once, and making pre-paration to receive Alastair if he were still alive. There was no room for him at the farm, where Ranald's wife had given birth to a child two days before. So with little Pòl, the herd-boy, she set out once more, leaning often upon the lad's shoulder ; and wondering if, after all, God were going to let her be of some service before he led her through the blind way till her hand should slip into that of her husband.

Before they left the farmstead, the Macraes had provided themselves with lanterns, a long rope, and a pine-torch dipped in tar.

As they neared the summit of Craig-Geal, they could hear the frenzied barking of Ghaoth in the darkness down by the sea—loud when caught on an eddy of wind and borne upward, scarce audible when overborne by the moan and boom and ever recurrent breaking surge of the advancing tide.

At the dark circular exit of the cavern, they waved lanterns and shouted themselves hoarse: but without seeing aught, or winning response.

Angus Macrae silently drew back, rose, and lit the pine-torch. Flaring abruptly into the dark before a gust of wind, it was like a blood-red wound in the flank of some vast black creature of night.

Having fastened the torch to the rope, he swung it far down the narrow funnel, up which came the smell of wrack and sea-damp and an obscure, muffled sound.

Still there was nothing visible. No shout followed the sudden glare.

The old man stood silent, craning forward with brooding eyes; for now he was thinking of the two sons he had lost. With a shudder, he moved slowly back and turned to Ranald.

"Will you go down?"

"Aye, father, that I will: if you will breathe the holy word before me and after me. The kelpie . . . the Sea-Woman . . . won't catch *me*, for I am sure of hand and foot."

"So your brother Sheumais thought."

Ranald hesitated, looked at the cave-mouth, then at his father.

"Is it true Sheumais died in *that* way?"

"It is true. The tide hemmed him in, and a heavy sea foamed at the mouth of the cavern. There was no chance but to gain some ledge high above the Sea-Woman's Pool. He did gain a hold on a ledge, for long afterwards we found his knife on it. Then the accursed kelpie rose out of her lair and took him by the legs, and pulled him down, and tore him, and broke the bones of him,—my son, my son, my beautiful Sheumais!"

As the old man spoke, his voice had grown louder, his tone more intense; and at the last the memory of his loss so wrought upon him that, with a sudden cry, he dashed forward and whirled one of the lanterns into the dark, echoing chasm.

"Let me go, let me go," he cried, as his son tried to withhold him. "If she must have one of us again, let it be me! Let go, boy! You have your wife and child: and I am old, and have lost Sheumais and Andras and the mother who bore them!"

Without a word, Ranald desisted. The old man went on his knees, crawled forward, and pulled up the flaming torch. Then, having fastened the rope round his waist and secured a lantern to his belt, he slipt over the edge and began the descent, cautiously feeling his way with his feet as he went.

As he reached further and further into the darkness, he wondered why he heard no more the barking of Ghaoth. A grim thought came into his mind: the dog had been caught by the Sea-Woman, and was even now drifting round and round in her pool, strangled, with glazed, protruding eyes.

At last, both sight and sound told him that he was nearly over the abyss— sight and sound, and his careful counting of the steps in his descent.

The tidal wash, the heavy lapse and then heavier resurge, with the rush and cataract-roar of the seas as they fell far down into the chasm, assailed his ears continuously. Peering down, he could see the foam upon the flood, as it swept ravening round the cave and then fell headlong into the abyss, above which was a misty pulsating whiteness, the send and spray of tons of whirled water.

There was almost no need to descend further, he thought. The strongest swimmer, if caught in that inrush, would be swept irresistibly into the horrible cauldron where the Sea-Woman brewed her spells of storm and disaster.

There was but one chance for Alastair; if, in truth, he were in the cave at all and still alive. A little way below where the isleman stood, there were three or four broad ledges of which even the lowest would still be unswept by the sea. He dreaded to descend; for it was on the first of those ledges that his son, Sheumais, had been dragged, screaming, into the abyss. With a muttered prayer, however—a prayer that was half an incantation—he once more slowly crawled downward.

When he came to the third ledge, he stopped, crouched, and peered downward and forward.

For a moment, his brain swung.

What was it that he saw? What fantasy was this? what horrible caprice of his eyes? Had Ghaoth slain the kelpie, and was he now perishing there with his teeth fixt in the neck of the Sea-Woman?

For Ghaoth, and no other, was the dog that crouched on the lowest ledge; and a woman it was who lay beside him, upheld at the neck by his strong teeth.

He saw the gleam in the dog's eyes, fixt upon him unwaveringly. He understood their appeal. Slowly he unfastened and raised his lantern.

When he recognised Lora, he knew intuitively what had happened. With uplifted arm, he let the light fall all around—above weedy, sea-swept boulders, and the dark, inward-moving flood, broken here and there into a seethe of foam that shone ghastly white in the lantern-glow.

There was no sign of Alastair.

It was clear he was either already swept into the chasm, or had been sucked seaward in the undertow.

With utmost care, Macrae stepped on to the lowest ledge.

Stooping, he looked intently in Lora's white face. Then he put his hand to her heart. He fancied he felt it beat, but could not be sure. Drawing a flask from his pocket, he poured some of the contents down her throat, then upon her temples and breast, with rough hand laving the spirit across the bosom which, cold as it was, had not the unmistakable chill of death. A new strength came to the old man. He had lost all fear now, and had no other thought but to save this poor creature who had already looked on the face of Death, and nigh perished with the horror of it.

Taking her in his arms, he was swiftly securing her to his body by the rope, when he was startled to see Ghaoth, who had at once let go his hold, leap into the surge and swim seaward.

The dog went to its doom, he knew, in a vain quest for Alastair. With a moment's sigh, he turned to what he had to do.

An arduous and perilous climb it was ere the old islesman at last neared the summit, and felt Ranald grasp him by the shoulder and help him and his burden over the edge.

He would have swooned from the long strain upon him, had not his son hastily put the flask of whiskey to his mouth and imperatively bid him drink.

As soon as he could breathe freely once more, he recounted what had happened. The young man wanted to go down at once into the cave and seek for Alastair, in the hope that he might still be swimming in the open or be somewhere afloat, and that Ghaoth might reach him and bring him to the spot where the dog had guarded Lora—almost from the moment, though of course neither Macrae nor his son knew aught of this, when the first ledge-sweeping wave broke upon the sleepers and reft asunder their impotent weedy bonds.

But of this project Angus Macrae would hear nothing further. Was his son mad, he asked him, to believe that Alastair could still be alive, since he was visible nowhere?

" No," he added, " he is in the deep sea by now, or lies gript by the Woman in her hole. But, Ranald, if to search for his body you are so fain, you can go down later. May be you will find the dog, though I think neither you, nor I, nor any one else will ever see dog or man again. Meanwhile, take up this poor soul and carry her to Widow Ealasaid's."

"She is big with child," whispered the young man, as awe-struck he wrapped Lora in his warm plaid and raised her in his arms.

"Aye : God have pity on this lost ewe and her poor, wee lammie. Be careful, Ranald, be tender— aye, as tender as if she were your own Cairistine, and the babe that is now moving within her were blood of your blood and bone of your bone."

In silence, and as swiftly as possible, the two men, with their still more silent burden, crossed the slopes of the ridge and ascended the grassy, boulder-strewn brae. In due time, they were met at the door by Ealasaid.

With a low, crooning wail, the old woman helped to lay Lora on the bed in the inner room. She had already warmed the clothes, and had poured boiling water in a tub, with hot flannels for swathing. All island-women act thus on any hint of accident, for the hunger of the sea is the cause of nearly every disaster for them and their loved ones. Besides—had not Duncan Bàn once been brought home, and all this and more done for him, though the chill upon him was not that of the sea only ?

Suddenly she saw there was no time to lose.

"Quick, quick, Pòl," she cried : "take a lantern and run like the wind across to the clachan, and tell Mrs. Mary Maclean that she is to come here at once, for Alastair Macleod is dead and his wife is lying here in labour, and that the last pains may come upon her speedily."

The boy hesitated a moment, glanced at his grandfather, and then fled into the night, heedless of any lantern, and sure-footed as a goat.

Finding that he could be of no use, and that Mrs. MacAodh wished only his father to remain, Ranald Macrae slipped quietly away : and in a brief while had reached the cave-entrance, descended, and searched vainly for any trace of either Alastair or the dog.

To Ealasaid's unceasing care Lora owed her life. The old woman seemed to have grown years younger. A new strength was in her arm, a new light in her worn eyes, a new spirit in her frail body. With deft hands, she rubbed the skin aglow, wrapped warm flannels about the limbs, breathed into breast and back, soothed the convulsive strainings of the sides and heavy womb, fed the unconscious sufferer with sips of broth and warmed spirit, and often the while kissed the poor faintly quivering lips. It seemed to her as if her heart swam in tears ; but, with the unnoticed heroism of women, she let no grief overmaster her, no flagging of mind or body usurp her will.

In the outer room Angus Macrae sat, intent at first upon the keeping up of the fire and the fulfilment of Ealasaid's divers commands. Then, nigh an hour later, when through the open doorway he heard a strange moaning from the inner room, he sat down by the low, rude table, and, taking the Gaelic Bible which lay there, began in a slow, monotonous voice to read from the page which caught his eye as he opened the book :—

" I returned, and saw under the sun, that the race is not to the swift, nor the battle to the strong, neither yet bread to the wise, nor yet riches to men of understanding, nor yet favour to men of skill ; but time and chance happeneth to them all. For man also knoweth not his time : as the fishes that are taken in an evil net, and as the birds that are caught in the snare, even so are the sons of men snared in an evil time, when it falleth suddenly upon them."

As 'he read steadfastly onward through this moving last chapter of *Ecclesiastes*, his voice rose, and took a rhythmic chant, and filled the room, as a rising wind fills a valley set among the hills.

But when he had read :

" As thou knowest not what is the way of the wind, nor how the bones do grow in the womb of her that is with child ; even so thou knowest not the work of God who doeth all ———"

he stopped abruptly, for he heard a

114

sound at the outer door, and guessed, even before he saw her, that the comer was Mrs. Maclean.

Angus rose, and took her hand. Then, seeing the speechless sorrow in her eyes, he let go his hold of her, and, bowing his head, did not lift up his eyes again till Mary had entered the inner room.

He knew that, with these two women there, all would go well with Lora, if it were ordained that she was to live. But he feared that death was already entered in at the door; and he knew not what passionate sorrow might come upon and undo those who ministered to the woman who even now was in those pains of labour that ere morn should end in the birth of a child. Long he sat brooding. Then, weary of his vigil, once more he began to read, resuming with the verse where he had been interrupted :—

" Even so, thou knowest not the work of God who doeth all.

" In the morning sow thy seed, and in the evening withhold not thine hand : for thou knowest not which shall prosper, whether this or that, or whether they both shall be alike good."

Looking up, he saw Ealasaid standing at the door, a wonderful light on her old face.

"It lives," she said simply. "Mary said that the child would certainly be born dead; but it lives. She says now it has the shadow upon it, and must die ere long; but they told me that my own little blossom was strong, and would live: . . . and even as they were wrong, wrong also may Mary Maclean be."

Hearing a call, she turned, and went within.

The old islesman muttered for a while, with bent head and closed eyes. Then he began to·read again :—

"Truly the light is sweet, and a pleasant thing it is for the eyes to behold the sun."

"Hush !"

It was Mary who spoke. She had that in her face which made him rise.

"Hush, Angus Macrae. Truly, the eyes are the delight of the body, but this is not the time for the bitterness of that saying. Never for this child, that is born in the shadow of death, and can itself live but a brief while, shall there be the sweet light of which you speak, nor the pleasantness of beholding the sun, nor the way of the day betwixt rise and set."

"Is the child blind?"

"Ay . . . blind . . . blind."

"And weakling?"

" Ay."

"And she?"

"God hath given her strength to endure."

" Does she know all that has happened?"

"If she did, she would be with Alastair. Her mind is dazed. She is as one distraught. My friend, read no more to-night. Go home now, and God be with you. Bring on the morrow what tidings you have."

Soon after the departure of the old man, a great stillness fell upon the house. Lora slept in a stupor like unto death. The child lay upon her breast, as a frail flower drifted there by a chance wind. Ealasaid sat by the bed watching. Mary knelt against it, crying silently.

Towards dawn, Mrs. Maclean rose, and looked out upon the chill dusk. When she came back, she kneeled again ; and, in a low voice, repeated a strange Celtic " Prayer of Women " :—

O Spirit, that broods upon the hills
And moves upon the face of the deep,
And is heard in the wind,
Save us from the desire of men's eyes,
And the cruel lust of them,
And the springing of the cruel seed
In that narrow house which is as the grave
For darkness and loneliness .   .   .

That women carry with them with shame,
and weariness, and long pain,
Only for the laughter of man's heart,
And the joy that triumphs therein,
And the sport that is in his heart,
Wherewith he mocketh us,
Wherewith he playeth with us,
Wherewith he trampleth upon us . . .
Us, who conceive and bear him;
Us, who bring him forth;
Who feed him in the womb, and at the breast,
and at the knee:
Whom he calleth Mother,
And Mother again of his wife and children:
When he looks at our hair, and sees it is white;
And at our eyes, and sees they are dim;
And at our lips, straitened out with long pain;
And at our breasts, fallen and seared as a
barren hill;
And at our hands, worn with toil;
And, seeing, seeth all the bitter ruin and
wreck of us—
All save the violated womb that curses him—
All save the heart that forbeareth . . *for*
pity—
All save the living brain that condemneth
him—
All save the spirit that shall not mate with
him—
All save the soul he shall never see
Till he be one with it, and equal;
He who hath the bridle, but guideth not;
He who hath the whip, yet is driven;
He who as a shepherd calleth upon us,
But is himself a lost sheep, crying among the
hills!
O Spirit, and the Nine Angels who watch us,
And Thy Son, and Mary Virgin,
Heal us of the Wrong of Man:
We, whose breasts are weary with milk,
Cry, cry to Thee, O Compassionate!

Ealasaid trembled. She had never heard words such as these before, and was afraid ; yet even more of the strange intensity in the voice of Mrs. Maclean, in the shine of her usually quiet eyes.

" God be with you, Mary Maclean."

"And with you, Ealasaid MacAodh."

Therewith Mrs. Maclean arose, looked at Lora to see if she still slept, and then went into the adjoining room, where she seated herself before the hot glow of the peats ; and, as the day broke, read below her breath in the third chapter of the Book of Job.

Weeks passed, and there was no word of Alastair. For twenty days after the coming of the child, Lora lay distraught, knowing no one about her, though oftentimes looking long and lovingly in the eyes of Mary, whose face had won again an exceeding peace, and who went, as of yore, girt about with a beautiful silence as with a garment.

But on the last day of the third week, Lora awoke in her right mind. Mary had given the frail, blind babe to young Cairistine Macrae to suckle. This was well; for had Lora looked upon it on that day, she would have died.

Nevertheless, in a brief while thereafter she knew all. It seemed strange, both to Mary and Ealasaid, that she did not appear greatly to care. She had that in her heart which would have enlightened them; but grief, as well as madness or evil, has its cunning, and so she veiled her purpose in absolute secrecy.

Not a sign of Alastair! This was what she could not accept. Till his body, or some trace of it, were found, she said she would not return with Mary to her home. Nothing, however, repaid the most scrupulous search: no clue was gained—unless the discovery of the body of Ghaoth, caught in a trawling net one night a mile seaward, could be called a clue.

On that day of agony when she had at last looked on the face of her child, and knew it stricken with frailty and blind for all its days, and heritor perhaps of that curse which had caused her to sin and incur this punishment, she had made a covenant with herself to go down as soon as she could to the shore, at low tide, and with her child follow Alastair into that abyss in the cavern where she felt assured he had been swept by the sea.

Two weary weeks passed before an opportunity came. One afternoon,

Mary went across Innisròn, so as to reach the clachan and meet the *Clansman* for somewhat she expected : and as she was to come back with Ranald Macrae, and he was not to return till after dark, Lora felt secure.

Early in the evening, she sent Ealasaid on a message to Parlan Macalister's wife, who lived in a cottage about a mile along the shore. beyond the promontory of Ardfeulan.

It was a lovely evening in mid-July. The moon was at the full, and made a golden dust upon the isle and a glory of pale gold upon the sea.

As she went once more down the hollow of the moonflowers — not so dense now as then, and many withered by the heat of the sun and the month-long drought—she stopped again and again, overcome by the heat even of the dusk.

In her ears was the bewildered, plaintive cry of the lapwings : and, as an undertone, the low, soft chime—the long, sweet ululation of the myriad-swung bell of the sea.

She was weary when she reached the shore. An unspeakable horror of the cavern came upon her, and she turned and went slowly towards the long sandy tract that stretched beyond the base of the hollow. There she laid the child gently down in the soft sand at her feet, and seated herself on a low rock.

After all, was it worth while to seek Death, when Death had already whispered that the little one was to be his own so soon, and had stealthily removed all but the last barriers that guarded her own poor life?

Would God not be even more wroth with her — punish her even more heavily; though this, indeed, seemed impossible?

How lovely that vast ocean veiled in violet dusk, save where lit gloriously with moonlight: how full of alluring peace, she thought, that wave-whisper all around her.

Surely the music was woven into a song that was dear and familiar in her ears?

She turned her head away from the sea, and looked idly along the sand: though, as she did so, the vague strain ceased.

Then Lora stood, trembling in a great awe, and with a passionate hope in her eyes, in her heart, at the very springs of life.

In the moonshine, she saw a tall figure moving slowly towards her, naked-white, and walking with a proud mien. The erect body, the flashing eyes, the grace and beauty, were those of a king—of a king among men: and as a king the naked figure was crowned, with moonflowers and yellow sea-poppies woven into his gold-sheen hair.

Suddenly he saw her. He stood as though wrought in impassioned stone. The moonshine fell full upon his white skin, upon the beauty of his face, upon the flower-tangle wherewith he had crowned himself.

Then, without a sound, he turned and fled like the wind, and vanished into the gloom that lay beyond the dusk.

And Lora, lifting the child and staggering homeward, knew that she had seen Alastair.

VI.

IT was not till many weeks later that
the way of Alastair's escape from
death became known.

On that dark night when he had
lain down to die, the wave which fell
across Lora and himself, and tore
asunder the bonds she had woven, was
followed by no other for a time : other-
wise, the end of both would have been
attained. But so great was the shock,
that his apathy of mind and body
was rudely broken. The tired blood
stung in his veins ; the instinct of life
was as a flame of fire that consumed
all the stupor due to the sea-fruit he
had eaten — an instinct that wrought
him to a passion of effort.

Shaken and trembling, he staggered
to his feet. Nothing but a profound
darkness beyond, behind, above : a
darkness filled with the voices of the
wind, the seething tide, wave falling

over wave, billow leaping after billow and tearing it into a yeast of foam— itself to stagger the next moment, and struggle and strangle furiously in a cloud of spray ere flung a dead mass upon the shore.

He had no remembrance of Lora, of what had brought them here, of the grave that was ready where the Sea-Woman watched.

But fear was left to him : and when he was aware of something moving across the ledges to his left, and heard it splash through the tide-wash in its effort to reach him, he gave a terrified cry, and dashed seaward to escape the grip of the kelpie.

Stumbling, he fell heavily forward. But it was into deep water ; and, powerful swimmer as he was, he fought the surge, and so was not thrown back upon the rocks till, unwittingly, he was caught in a cross-current and swept southward on the backs of the reeling sea-horses.

A horrible tumult was in his ears. The darkness was upon him as a heavy hand. As idle flotsam, the waves swung him backward and forward.

A deathly cold beset his limbs ; then utter weariness. His hands ceased to propel, and only automatically and instinctively kept him afloat.

Yet even now, at the last extremity, when memory was no more, terror remained.

There was something swimming near, something moving towards him through the dark.

The next moment he threw up his hands, overcome by the sickness of fear and a fatigue that he could no longer withstand. As he sank, he was conscious of a body surging up against his; of a hot breath against his face; of a gasping whine against his ear. Then in a flash he recognised, or by instinct divined, that it was Ghaoth who had followed into the darkness, and was there to save him.

The dog had indeed followed, having but an hour ago escaped from the byre where Ian Maclean had risen from his sleep to let him out because of his ceaseless whining. He had raced across the island, and along Alastair's and Lora's track, till he found them where they lay. Thence, after seeing the two whom he loved lying silent and motionless in a way that made him whine with fear, and knowing, as faithful dogs do know, that he must win help without delay, he had sped back to the nearest cottage. Once convinced that old Ealasaid was following to succour those whom he had left, he had sprung away again through the moonflowers, and had reached the entrance to the cave after fierce baffling with the tide-race. Just as Alastair had risen and was staggering towards the sea, Ghaoth had caught sight of him, and had plunged without hesitation into the black bewilderment of waters which had swallowed up the friend whom he loved with his life.

Fortunately, the spent swimmer was still near the shore — nearer, even, than when he had first fallen ; for he was now close to the headland of Craig-Geal, and was already in shallow water, which swung on to a long shelf of sand lying against the entrance to another of the innumerable caverns of that side of the island. But here the sea, though at full-flood it covered the sand and moved its hungry lip for a few feet within, did not enter, as a beast of prey halting unassuaged at the entrance to its lair.

Ghaoth had gripped him by the hair of his neck, and was now struggling to reach the shore. Man and dog were still flung to and fro by the waves ; but the living sport of the sea was no longer separate. With Ghaoth's help, Alastair made renewed, if despairing, efforts.

Suddenly his feet touched the ground for a moment. Then, with a staggering

rush, having shaken himself free of the
dog, he gained the shore, stumbled
blindly up the low shelve of the sound,
and fell unconscious among the soft,
powdery grit, midway in the wide
half-roofless hollow known as the
Cave of the Sùlaire, from the solan
geese which often congregated there
in the blinding snow-storms of winter.

Ghaoth stood panting beside him
awhile. At last, with a low whine, the
dog pressed his muzzle against the
white face in the white sand; turned
aside, whined again, and came back
with lolling tongue. Then, suddenly,
he sprang away into the darkness, and
back into the drowning surge, with all
his loyal, loving heart—beautiful love
of the dumb animal-soul that God
heedeth and cherisheth no less than
that other wandering fire He hath
placed in the human—eager to baffle
with drift and billow till he reached
the cavern once more, in time to
save Lora, of whose body he had
caught a glimpse as he dashed after
Alastair.

In time, and no more. He had not
long rescued Lora, who, also, had been
partially roused by the shock of the
breaking wave. She had been half-
standing, half-leaning against the higher
ledge to which, with difficulty and in

blind instinct, she had clung ; but, as Ghaoth reached her, she sank wearily and lay back against the dog, dreaming she had waked in terror, but was now safe in Alastair's arms.

It was thus that Angus Macrae discovered them. Long afterwards, the isleman recalled how he had seen the dog leap back into the darkness. Whether Ghaoth failed to reach the Cave of the Sùlaire, and was carried seaward by a current ; or whether his strength failed him in his last effort, and he was swung lifelessly from wave to wave ; whatever the first word of his fate was, the last was the finding of his sea-mangled body in the trawl-net of a fisherman more than a mile oceanward from Innisròn.

When Alastair woke, an hour or more after dawn, he remembered nothing of what had happened. His memory, though not killed, was clouded by his madness ; and, doubtless, the shock of what he had gone through, with the action of the mermaid's fruit, had further weakened it.

He rose and looked about him wonderingly. Around, were the precipitous rocks ; beyond, the sea stretched far into the morning mists, calm, with a silver sparkle in the south-

east, and turquoise - blue elsewhere,
except in green straits under the
shadow of the isle, till it faded into
opal and dove-grey where the veils of
mist slowly dispersed, re-wove, lifted,
in-wove, and sank to the wave again,
or sailed indefinitely away.

Though he could still recall nothing
of the past night, he recognised, as
soon as he stepped from the cave and
went down by the sea-marge, the head-
land of Craig-Ruaidh and that of Craig-
Geal just behind him. His one wish
was to hide, so that none should see
him. His fantasy led him to seek
remote places, and to fear the face of
his fellows.

Turning towards the sun, he looked
scrutinisingly along the coast. Some-
where beyond Craig-Geal, he remem-
bered vaguely, there was another hollow
which led to a series of intricate and
unexplored caves, perilous places of
evil repute among the islanders.

If he were to go there . . . but
at that moment his wandering gaze
lighted upon an object moving black
in the shine of the sea.

Was it a whale sunning itself, or a
pollack moving idly after the liath?
Then he saw that it was a boat—one
of many torn from moorings or swept
from the beach by the recent gale.

So methodical were his actions, that none seeing him would believe his mind was so darkly veiled, that his reason was only partially in exercise.

Having taken off his coat, he wrapt it round a heavy stone and threw the bundle far into the sea. Then he thrust his boots into a cranny in a fissured boulder that at full flood was covered.

A few seconds later he was in the water, swimming swiftly towards the derelict.

While he neared the boat, amid a sheen of sparkling foam as he urged his way through the sun-dazzle which lay upon that part of the sea, he broke intermittently into a mournful Gaelic chant, but with words so incoherent, and with interjections so wild and strange, that the fishermen on a coble, hid in the mist a few fathoms away, believed they listened to a sea-kelpie, or to that vague object of their pro-foundest dread known as "the thing that hides beneath the boat." They were southward bound; but at that forlorn wailing they hauled down their flapping sail, and, with their oars, made all haste northerly to their island or mainland haven. Not a man among them would have persevered in that voyage on that day.

Alastair heard the sound of the oar-wash, and ceased his fitful chant. It must, he thought, be dead seamen rowing to and fro, looking for the newly drowned to take their places as warders of the treasures and keepers of the secrets which lie among the weed-tangle and sunless caverns of the deep. At the thought, he laughed loud, but mirthlessly; and the echo of his laughter, falling against the ears of the fishermen, added to their horror and consternation.

With his hands gripping the gun-wale, he swayed for some time to and fro, fascinated by the lustrous green beneath the keel—green in the sunlit spaces as leaves of the lime in April, and in the lower as emerald lapsing into jade, and then as jade passing into the gloom of pines at dusk.

At last he raised himself on the water, bending the gunwale low, and half fell, half crawled into the boat. Indifferently, he noticed that it was named *Fionnaghal.* Clearly it had drifted away from moorings; for not only were oars and sail-enveloped mast lying taut under the thwarts, but a rope trailed from the bow far down into the water.

He rowed for some time. At last, becoming weary, or perhaps puzzled by the mists which crept behind and all

around him, he desisted. A flurry of
air struck his right cheek. Instinc-
tively he put up the palm of his hand
to feel if the wind were coming from
the south-east or the south-west. Then,
adjusting the mast and setting the sail,
he seated himself at the tiller.

Eddy followed eddy, and soon a
breeze blew freshly from the south-
east. By the time the *Fionnaghal* was
three or four miles to the north-west
of Innisròn, there was not a mist
upon the sea. Immeasurably vast it
stretched; blue, or glittering in a dia-
mond-sparkle sheen, or wimpling over
in violet hollows, with the white lambs
beginning to collect and leap merrily
onward in the pathway of the sun.

Alastair became drowsy with the
warmth of the glow upon his back
and the chime of the sea-music. Long
before noon he slept. For hours the
boat went idly adrift.

When he woke, he saw an island
less than half - a - mile to starboard.
Looking northward, he could descry
nothing but sea; to the westward,
nothing but sea; nothing but sea to
the southward. Far eastward, a dim
blue line of hills rose above the hori-
zon : here and there—lying apparently
against it, and scarce bigger to his eye
than the gannets and sea-mews which

flew overhead—two or three patches of amethyst. These were the isles he had left, though he did not recognise them : Ithona, most westerly ; Innisròn, remote in the south-east ; I-na-Tril-leachan-tràbad, lost in its northerly purple-greys.

Though the words brought no meaning to him, or awakened nothing beyond mere visual reminiscence, his lips, as he looked at the island he was now approaching, framed its name, " I-Mònair."

Heedless of the fact that he was running straight upon a shore set with reefs like gigantic teeth, he tautened the sail and let the boat rush forward, and was almost havened when, with a grinding rip, the *Fionnaghal* stopped, filled, leaned over, and hung upon a jagged reef, as a dead body suspended on the horn that has gored it.

Alastair was thrown forward by the shock. Bruised and stunned, he lay motionless for a few seconds while the water poured over him. Then, rising, and casting a keen glance around, he stepped on to the reef, sprang thence to a rock nearer the shore, and thence to the shore itself.

As he left the boat, it split. The larger half went drifting on the tide.

He sat down to watch idly for the disappearance of the few planks which remained. Suddenly, without cause, he rose, stared wildly at the sea and along the shore on either hand, and then moved rapidly inland—often casting furtive glances behind him, now on the one side, now on the other.

No other lived on I-Mònair than a shepherd and his wife; and they only through the summer months. Sometimes weeks passed by without their seeing another soul : without other sign of the world of men than the smoke of a steamer far upon the horizon, or the brown patches in the distance when the herring-trawlers ventured ocean-ward.

No wonder, then, that Fearghas McIan gave a cry of astonishment, that was partly fear, when he saw a man walking swiftly towards him . . . . a man who appeared to have dropped from the clouds; for, looking beyond the stranger, the shepherd could see no sign of trawler, wherry, or boat of any kind.

"Diònaid, Diònaid," he cried to his wife, who had come to the door of the cottage to see if he were at hand for his porridge; "Trothad so . . . . bi ealamh, bi ealamh : quick, quick, come here."

They stood together as Alastair slowly drew near. When he was close, he stopped, looking at them curiously, and with an air as if he wondered who they were and why they were there.

"What is your name?" he asked quietly, looking at the shepherd.

"C'ainm' tha ort" he repeated, as the man stared at him in surprise and something of alarm.

"Fearghas McIan."

"And yours?" he asked of the woman.

"Diònaid McIan."

"Cò tha sin?" he added abruptly, pointing to the cottage: "who is there?"

"No one."

"I thought I saw some one come out, look at us, and go in again."

Fearghas and Diònaid glanced at each other with eyes of dread.

"C'aium' tha ort" asked the former, in turn.

Alastair looked at him, as if uncomprehendingly; and then, in a low, dull voice, said that he was tired; that he was hungry, and thirsty, and wet.

"Tha mi glé sgith; tha an t' acras orm; tha am pathadh orm; tha mi flìuch."

"How did you come here?"

"Tha mi glé sgith."

"Did you come in a boat? Where is the boat you came in?"

"Tha mi glé sgith."

"What is your name? Are you of the isles?"

"Tha mi glé sgith."

"What do you want with us here, on I-Mònair, where we do no wrong, O stranger who carrieth your sorrow in your eyes?"

"Tha mi glé sgith. Tha mi fliuch. Tha an t' acras orm. Tha mi glé sgith —tha mi glé sgith—tha mi glé sgith."

Alastair spoke in a strange, dull voice. It would have terrified Fearghas and Diònaid more, but that the stranger was so gentle in his manner, and had a look upon his face that awed while it reassured them.

"God has sent him," said Diònaid, simply. "The poor lad has not waked —he is in a dream. God do unto us as we do unto this waif from the sea. In His good time He will whisper in the closed ears, and the man will wake, and tell us who he is, and whence he came, and whither he would fain go."

"So be it, Diònaid. You have said the word, and a good word it is. When this man's hour has come, God will deliver him. Meanwhile, let us call him Donncha, after the boy we lost nigh upon six-and-twenty years ago, who might have been as tall and comely as this stranger that is now a stranger no more, but of us and one with us."

And so it was that, from that day, Alastair Macleod, unsought by any, and unrecognised because no one came near who might have known or guessed who he was, abode on I-Mònair with Fearghas the shepherd and his wife Diònaid.

He dwelt in peace. Through the long days he wandered about the shores. Often, in the gloaming, he sat on a rock and stared longingly across the waters for he knew not what, for some nameless boon he craved wit-lessly ; stared yearningly through the dusk for something that lay beyond, that, though unseen, brought a mist into his eyes, so that when he reached the peat-fire again, where Diònaid McIan awaited him, he often could not see to eat for awhile for the blur of his slow-falling tears.

Week succeeded changeless week. The sheep ceased to look up as he passed. The yellowhammers in the gorse sang even when he stopped brooding by the bush whereon they flitted from branch to branch, looking at him the while with quiet eyes.

It was in the sixth week, after a time of storm which had lapsed into another long spell of exquisite summer, that the dream came to its end.

Late one afternoon, a herring-trawler lay off I-Mònair. The skipper, a kinsman of Fearghas, came ashore to give and learn what news there was.

Alastair had come back about the usual time from one of his daylong rambles, and, as he approached the door, his quick ear had caught the sound of an alien voice.

Whether he overheard the shepherd tell his friend, in turn for the strange and moving tale of Alastair MacDiarmid Macleod, of Innisròn, of the strange visitor he and his wife nourished, with the surmise that he, Donncha, might be no other than the missing man ; or whether some other suggestion concerning his removal or identification alarmed him, no one ever knew.

But, in the cloudy dark of that night, when Rory McIan and his two mates, Dùghall and Eòghann, were drinking the crude spirit from Fearghas' illicit still, Alastair slipped into the small boat in which they had come ashore, and rowed softly away into the obscure and lonely wilderness of the sea.

Truly, as Diònaid said, God must have whispered in the closed ears, and told him whither to guide the boat, and when to rest while he let it drift, and when to take up the oars again. For, betwixt dawn and sunrise, the fugitive, oaring slowly out of a pearly haze, came abruptly upon the south-west of Innisròn.

With a cry of gladness, he leaned forward, shading with his right hand his eager eyes. He had recognised familiar features of shore and headlands. The whim took him to capsize the boat and swim ashore. In sudden excitement, he sprang to his feet. The little craft rocked wildly. The next moment Alastair had left the upturned keel to drift in the grey sea like a water-snake, and was swimming swiftly across the two or three hundred yards which lay between the island and the place where he had fallen.

When he reached the shore, he wandered slowly to and fro, his new-born energy having lapsed into a vague unrest. Aimlessly he leant now against one boulder, now against another. At last, the chill of his dripping clothes gave him active discomfort. He looked doubtfully on the slopes, then at the sea, then again at the slopes. With the strange impulsiveness of his disease, he turned abruptly ; with swift, stumbling steps, crossed the shore ; passed the ridges covered with sea-grass, and entered the shaws beyond. Thence he walked quickly up the corrie behind Craig-Geal. When he gained the upper end, the sunrise shone full upon him. Flinging first one wet garment from him, and then another, he was speedily naked—beautiful in his fair youth, with his white skin and tangle of yellow hair, which, as the sunrays blent with it, seemed to spill pale gold.

He laughed with pleasure; then raced to and fro for warmth. When tired, he stooped to pluck the thyme or tufts of gale. For awhile, he wandered thus circlewise, aimlessly happy.

The day came with heat, and hourly grew hotter. Alastair was glad to lie down in a shady place by a burn, and drowse through the long, warm hours. As the afternoon waned into gloaming, he rose, and, forgetful of or unheeding his discarded clothes, wandered idly northward by one of the many sheep-paths. It was late when, having woven for himself a crown of moonflowers into which he inserted afterwards a few yellow sea-poppies, he made his way down to the sea, and hungrily ate of what shell-fish he could gather—briny cockles from the sand, and whelks and mussels from the rocks.

At the coming of the moonlight across the water, he laughed low with joy. It was only in the darkness he heard that Voice in the sea which called, called, called, and terrified him so even while it allured him. The waves, dancing and leaping in the yellow shine and breaking into a myriad little cups and fleeting hollows, sang a song that filled him with joy.

Then it was that, with erect head, flashing eyes, and proud mien, crowned with moonflowers and sea-poppies, and beautiful in the comeliness of his youth, Alastair appeared before the startled eyes of Lora, who, for the second time, had come down to that shore to woo and win Death.

When, late that night, Mary Maclean returned, she found Lora in Ealasaid's arms, sobbing and moaning hysterically.

It was long ere she was able to learn the exact truth, and at first she doubted if Lora were not suffering from a hallucination. But as the young mother grew calm, and took up her frail babe and kissed it with tears, Mary was won to believe in at least the possibility that the vision was, if not of Alastair in the body, at any rate the wraith of him, allowed to be seen of Lora out of God's pity of her despair.

The night was too far gone for anything to be done straightway; but she promised to go forth with Lora at sunrise and see if that white, flower-crowned phantom walked abroad in the day, and was no mere fantasy of the moonshine.

She had fallen asleep when, at dawn, Lora aroused her.

Without a word, she rose from the chair, wrapped a shawl about her, and then, kissing Lora gently, looked at her with quiet, questioning eyes.

" What is it, Mary ? "

" You still believe that you saw Alastair . . . Alastair in the body ? "

" Yes."

" Then had you not better take the child with you ? I will carry the little one. If he should see it––perhaps he would. . . ."

" You are right, dear friend. God has put that thought into your mind."

A few minutes later, the two women passed out into the cold, fresh morning; Mary going first with the child, and keeping, wherever practicable, to the sheep-paths or to the barren ledges that ran out every here and there from the heather and bracken, and this because of the dews which lay heavily, giving a moon-white sheen to the grass, and sheathing every frond and leaf and twig as with crystal, glistening rainbow-hued.

They took a path that trailed above the hollow of the moonflowers, and led deviously shoreward by the side of Craig-Geal.

When they reached the summit of the grassy brae, where the path diverged, they looked long in every direction. Nowhere could they discern sign of any human being. Not a soul moved upon the upland moors; not a soul moved upon the boulder-strewn, rowan - studded slopes; not a soul moved by the margin of that dead-calm sea, so still that even the whisper of its lip was inaudible, though the faint aerial echo of the crooning of its primeval slumber-song slipt hushfully into the ear.

They were half-way down towards the shore when Mrs. Maclean, holding up a warning hand, stopped.

"What is it, Mary?" Lora whispered: "Do you see anything? Do you see him?"

"Look!" and, as she spoke, Mary pointed to a dip in the little glen.

Under a rowan, heavy with clusters of fruit, as yet of a ruddy brown touched here and there with crimson a white figure stooped, leaning over one of the pools wherein the falling burn slept and dreamed awhile ere it leaped again from ledge to ledge, or slipt laughing and whispering through time-worn channels.

He was like some beautiful creature of an antique tale. Even as a wild deer, he stooped and drank ; looked questioningly through the rowans and birches, and then across the bracken where the sunrays slid intricately in a golden tangle ; then, stooping again, again drank.

The sunlight was warm about him. His shoulders and back gleamed ivory-white, dusked flickeringly here and there with leaf-shadows. A shadowy green-gloom lay upon his curved breast and against his thighs, from the sheen of the water passing upward through the dense fern that overhung the stream.

"It is the young god," thought Mary ; " the young god who, Sheumais the Seer says, was born of human hope, weaned with human tears, taught by dreams and memories, and therewith given for his body, Beauty . . . and for his soul, Immortal Joy."

But aloud she murmured only, " It is he — the Beautiful One — of the *Domhan Tòir* ! "

Lora did not look at her; but below her breath whispered, "*It is Alastair.*"

Swiftly and silently, they moved forward.

So intent was Alastair, after he had quenched his thirst, upon what he saw or imagined in the pool beneath him, that he did not hear their steps till they were but a few yards away.

"*Alastair!*"

He lifted his head and listened.

"*Alastair!*"

The sudden fear passed from his eyes. A smile came into them, and his lips parted:

"Lora . . . Lorà bhàn . . . Lora, my beautiful gloom . . . my fawn . . . my little one . . ."

As he spoke, with low, caressing, yearning voice, he looked into the heart of the pool again, and stretched forward his arms longingly.

A sob behind him fell upon his ears. Startled, he sprang back.

For more than a minute, he looked intently at Lora and Mrs. Maclean. Then, slowly, some reminiscence worked in his brain. Slowly, too, the dark veil began to lift from his mind; slightly, and for a brief while at most.

"Mary!"

Mrs. Maclean made a step towards him, but stopped. The peace that was about her at all times breathed from her, and lay upon him. The benediction of her eyes upheld him.

Quietly she spoke, with her right hand pointing to the sobbing woman at her side.

" Alastair . . . this is Lora, who has sought you far, and now has found you."

" Lora ? Lora is dead ! She is a beautiful spirit, and sleeps in that pool under the rowan. She walked with me last night in the moonshine. She has a beautiful child that is our child. It is now a song, singing in the sunshine. I heard it at dawn, when I was listening to the stars calling one to another. It is a song of joy about the doorway of Pharais. I saw the golden doors open a brief while ago—the doors of Pharais. Our little child danced in the glory as a mote in a sunbeam. But Lora is dead."

" Hush ! Lora is not dead, but liveth. Lora is here. See, her tears run for you—her bosom heaves for you—her arms reach for you ! "

Slowly the dreamer advanced. He would not come quite close at first, but there was a wonderful new light in his eyes.

" Alastair ! Alastair ! It is I, Lora !
Come to me ! Come to me ! "

" If, indeed . . . if, indeed, you
are Lora . . . Lora, my joy . . .
where is our child whose soul I heard
singing in the sunshine over against
Tigh-na-Pharais ? "

Without a word, and swiftly, Lora
took her poor blind blossom from
Mary, and held the child towards him.

" It is God's gift to us, Alastair," she
added at last, seeing that he came no
nearer, and looked at the child wonder-
ingly.

He advanced slowly, till his breath
fell upon Lora's hands, and made her
heart strain with its passion. Stopping,
he stretched forth his right hand and
gently touched the sleeping face. A
sunray fell upon it. Then a smile grew
upon the little parted lips, as the spirit
of a flower might grow and bloom bodi-
less in dreamland.

Alastair smiled. With soft, caressing
hand, he smoothed the child's face and
little, uplifted arm. Then he took it
gently from its mother, kissed it, handed
it to Mary.

And having done this, he opened his
arms and said one word : " Lora ! "

None saw their return. Mrs. Mac-
lean went before them with the child,

and at once sent Ealasaid out to keep watch and ward against the coming of any one. Thereafter she swiftly made all ready for those whom God had lifted out of the grave.

But so weary was Alastair—so far spent by hunger, and fatigue, and exposure—that he could not put on the clothes laid ready for him. So Lora led him gently to bed ; and there, after he had swallowed a little broth and warm milk, he fell into a profound sleep which lasted till dark, and then, after a brief interval wherein he ate ravenously, till late on the morrow.

From that time forth, Alastair's madness took a new form. All of dark gloom, of dread or vague fear, went from him. His reason seemed to be a living energy again, though still bewilderingly distraught at times, and ever veiled.

Nevertheless, that day of his awakening after his long, life-saving slumber was the last wherein the things of his past and the affairs of the present were realities to him. Concerning these, he could listen to little and speak less ; and, again and again, his struggling thought became confused and his words incoherent.

Yet Lora learned enough to know what his one passionate wish was. Full well he knew that the end was not far from him ; but before he entered into the silence he might live many months ; and he longed to leave Innisròn. Beyond words, he longed to die in that little lonely isle of Ithona which was his sole heritage from his mother, and where he had been born ; for his father had brought his fair Eilidh there from his old gloomy castle at Dunvrechan for the travail that was her doom.

Upon Ithona no one dwelt other than an old islander whose fathers had been there before him for generations.

Sheumais Macleod was at once shepherd and fisherman, and caretaker of the long, low farmhouse : alone now, since the death of his wife at midsummer of that year. There was room and to spare for Alastair and Lora and the little one ; for Mary also—for Mrs. Maclean never dreamed of parting from these her children.

And thus it was arranged, ere dusk came and filled with violet shadows all the hollows that lay betwixt the cottage and the sea.

Three days thence, late on a hot afternoon scarce cooled by the breeze that moved soundlessly though steadily over the upland crags of Innisròn, a company of islanders was met at the

little western haven betwixt Ardfeulan
and Craig-Ruaidh. Every one on the
isle was there, indeed, except the one
or two who were weakly or in extreme
old age.

On the water, moored to a ledge, a
herring-trawler, the *Ellù*, lay with her
brown sail flapping idly. In the stern
sat Lora, with her child at her breast,
and beside her Mrs. Maclean. In the
waist, with a leg on either side of the
seat, Angus Macrae, who owned the
boat, leaned against the mast.

The islanders made a semi-circular
group. In the middle were six or
seven old men : on either side were the
younger men, women old and young,
and the children. Behind were the
collie dogs, squatted on their haunches
or moving restlessly to and fro.

Some mischance had made it im-
possible for Mr. Macdonald, the old
minister of these outer isles, to be
present. Father Manus, a young priest
of Iona, took his place, and had already
blessed the sea, and the *Ellù* that was
to voyage across it, and those who were
going away for ever from Innisròn, and
the weary hearts they carried with them,
and the sad hearts of those who were
gathered to see them go.

Alastair, tall, frail, with wild eyes
strangely at variance with the quiet

pallor of his face—and to many there scarce recognisable, so greatly had he altered—was bidding farewell to the elders one by one.

Not a word else was spoken by any than the familiar good-bye—*Beannachd leibh*. The hearts of all were too full.

At the last, Alastair came to where Ealasaid MacAodh stood, crying silently. He took her in his arms, and kissed her on the brow and then upon both eyes.

She watched him as he moved slowly down to the *Ellù*. He stepped on board, followed by Ranald Macrae, and sat down beside Lora, whose hand he took in his, and with the other stroked it gently.

As old Angus Macrae shook out the sail, Ealasaid suddenly fell on her knees, and, swaying to and fro, began a wailing lament :—

> *Tha mo latha goirid,*
> *Tha mo feasgar fada,*
> *O, oi, oi, tha cèo air a' bheinn,*
> *O, oi, oi, tha drùchd air an fheur!*

> My day is short,
> Long is my night—
> O, alas, alas, the mist upon the hill,
> O, alas, alas, the dew upon the grass !

Slowly the *Ellù* moved out from the haven.

Lora and Mary sat with bowed heads.
Alastair had turned and was staring
seaward, where a glory of gold and
scarlet was gathered against the going
down of the sun.

O, oi, oi, tha cèo air a' bheinn,
O, oi, oi, tha dr̀uchd air an fheur!

sang the islanders in a long, wailing
chant.

Suddenly the sail filled, became taut.
The boat moved swiftly before the
wind.

A deep silence fell upon all. Then
Griogair Fionnladh, the oldest of the
islesmen, raised the pipes from his
shoulder and began to play.

But the wild, mournful, plaintive air
was not the expected Lament of Fare-
well. It was the ancient Coronach for
the Dead.

One by one, every man doffed his
bonnet ; the white-haired elders bowing
their heads, and, with downcast eyes,
muttering inaudibly. Sobs were heard
and tears fell ; but no word was spoken.

When the sun set, the *Ellì* was far
on her way—a black speck in the
golden light. With the coming of the
gloaming, the islanders slowly dis-
persed. Soon there was none left,
save Fionnladh and Ealasaid.

For a long while thereafter upon

the twilight-water rose and fell, mingling with the solemn, rhythmic chant of the waves, the plaintive, mournful wail of the Coronach for those who have passed into the silence.

When that, too, had ceased, there was no sound that the sea heard not nightly, save the sobbing of the woman Ealasaid.

VII.

𝔚EEK after week, month after month, until nigh the end of the fourth, passed by on Ithona : and they who dwelt there took no heed of the passage of the days.

There are no hours for those who are beyond the rumour of that "time or chance" of which the Preacher speaks. Day grows out of night, and in night fulfilleth itself again : the stars succeed the diurnal march of the sun, and hardly are they lost in his glory ere they come again. Scarce distinguishable are the twilight of the dawn and the twilight of the eve : and even as the coming and going of these similar shadows are the appearance and evanishing of the shadows whom we know for our fellow-men, so little differing one from the other, individual from individual, people from people, race from race.

And even as a shadow, to those who abode on Ithona, was that world they had seen so little of, but of which they had yet known enough.

In that remote island, solitary even among the outer isles of which it was one of the most far-set in ocean, there was little to break the monotony of the hours. No steamer drew near, save at long intervals. The coastguard cutter arrived intermittently, but sometimes not for months, coming like an alien sea-bird, and as a strange bird of the seas going upon its unknown way again. Few even of the herring-trawlers sailed nigh, except in the late summer, when the mackerel came eastward in vast shoals.

Morning and noon, afternoon and evening, night and the passing of night, dawn and sunrise: these were the veils that seemed to curtain off this spot of earth. Storm followed calm; calm succeeded storm: the winds came and went: the tides rose and fell. In summer, the rains from the south; in autumn, the rains from the west; in winter, the rains from the north. Change followed change, but orderly as in processional array. The poppies reddened the scanty fields of rye;

the swallows and martins haunted the island-ways; the wild rose bloomed, as with white and pink sea-shells made soft and fragrant. Then a little while, and the ling grew purple at the passing of the roses; the hawks swung in the wind when the swallows had vanished; the campions waved where the poppies had fallen; the grey thistle usurped the reaped grain. In summer, the Weaver of Sunshine rested there; there, during the equinox, the Weaver of the Winds abode; in winter, the Weaver of the Snow made a white shroud for the isle and wove a shimmering veil for the dusking of the sea. And as one spring was like another spring, and one autumn like another autumn, so was one year like another year, in the coming and in the going.

Save for the encroaching shadow of death, there was nothing to mark the time for the dwellers on Ithona. Mary was aware that not Alastair only, but Lora, was becoming frailer week by week. Lora, as well as Mary, knew that the child's face grew more wan and thin almost day by day. Old Sheumais Macleod was weary at heart with the pity of all that he saw. Only Alastair was happy, for he dreamed; and his dream was of the loveliness of earth and sea and sky, of the pathway that came down from heaven at sunrise and led back at nightfall through the avenue of the stars to the very gates of Pharais. More happy, too, grew the others as the autumn waned, and the golden peace of St. Martin's aftermath lay upon sea and land; for their eyes saw more and more through the dreaming eyes of Alastair, more and more clearly they heard strains of the music that haunted his rapt ears.

Daily he went about clad with dream: a strange sweetness in his voice, a mystery upon his face. His eyes no longer brooded darkly; there was in them a bright light as of a cloudless morning.

If, months ago, God had filled with dusk the house of the brain, it was now not the dusk of coming night, but of the advancing day. Fantasies beset him often, as of yore, but never with terror or dismay. The moorland tarn held no watching kelpie: instead, he heard the laughter of the fairies as they swung in the bells of the foxglove; the singing of an angel where the wind wandered among the high corries; whispers and sighs of fair spirits in the murmur of leaves, or falling water, or chime of the waves.

Sometimes Lora walked or lay beside him for hours, listening to his strange

speech about the things that he saw—
things too lovely for mortal vision, but
ultimately as real to her as to him.
Hope came back to her; and then
Peace; and, at the last, Joy.

When not with Lora, he loved well
to be with Mary or with Sheumais.

In the eyes of the former he would
sometimes look for a long time, seeing
there the secret home of peace, and per-
haps, deeper, the unveiled beauty of
the serene and lovely soul.

Sheumais he had loved from child-
hood. The old islesman had never
once been on the mainland, though in
his youth he had sailed along its end-
less coasts. Tall and strong he was,
despite his great age ; and his eyes
were the eyes of a young man who
hears his first-born laughing and croon-
ing against its mother's breast. Igno-
rant as he was of the foreign tongue of
the mainland, ignorant of books, and
unable to read even a verse in the
Gaelic Scriptures of which he knew so
many chapters by heart, he was yet
strong in knowledge and wise in the
way of it beyond most men. For he
knew all that is to be known concern-
ing the island and the surrounding sea,
and what moved thereon and lived
therein ; and, in his humbleness and
simplicity, he saw so deep into the

human heart and into the mystery of the soul, that he was not ashamed to know he was man, nor to pray to God to guide him through the shadows.

It was from Sheumais that Alastair, in boyhood and youth, had learned much, not only of his store of legends and ancient runes and old Celtic poetry, but also of that living poetry which makes the heart of the Gael more tender than that of other men, and his brain more wrought with vision. From him he had first heard how that for one to have died is to have "gone into the silence;" that for an old man or woman to pass away in extreme age is to "have the white sleep;" that for a fisherman to drown is for him to have "the peace of the quiet wave."

Sheumais had filled his brain with lovely words—lovely in themselves and their meaning; but he had made his clansman a poet by one thing that he did and said.

For once, after Alastair had returned to the West from the University in St. Andrew's, he went to Ithona to stay for some weeks. At sunrise on the morrow of his arrival, on his coming out upon the grass which sloped to the shore a few yards away, he saw Sheumais standing, with his wide, blue bonnet in his hand, and the sun shining full upon his mass of white hair—not praying, as at first Alastair thought, but with a rapt look on his face, and with glad, still-youthful eyes gazing lovingly upon the sea.

" What is it, Sheumais ? " he had asked ; and the old islesman, turning to him with a grave smile, had answered :

"Morning after morning, fair weather or foul, after I have risen from my prayers and ere I have broken my fast, I come here and remove my hat and bow my head, with joy and thanksgiving, before the Beauty of the World."

From that day, the world became a new world for Alastair.

In the quietude of dusk—and day by day the dusk came sooner and the dawn later — Mary would sometimes sing, or Sheumais repeat some favourite Ossianic *duan*, or chant a fugitive song of the isles. But, towards the close of November, a silence fell more and more upon all. Each had grown a little weary with the burden of life: all knew Who it was that was coming stealthily across the waters, and for whom first.

It was on the dawn of December that the child died. It seemed to lapse from life as an ebbing wavelet from a pool.

The evening before, Alastair had

carried the little one to the shore. He had never understood that the child's eyes were sealed, and often thought that it slept when it was really awake. When he came to a favourite pool of his, that at low tide was wont to flush with any red light spilled across the wave, he held his tiny burden up, laughing and crooning to it.

" Look, my pretty one," he would murmur, " that red light is the blood of your elder brother. Fair is He, the white Christ. He has put that there to show that He loves you." Or, again, he would kneel, and with one hand warily move aside the bladder-wrack and other sea-weeds ; and then, pointing into the translucent water, would tell the blind sleeper to look into the heart of the pool and he would see, far down beyond a vast vista of white columns, flight after flight of shining golden stairs, which led at last to a great gate flashing like the sea in the noon-dazzle. And at the gate was a little child like unto himself, singing a sweet song ; and just within the gate was a beautiful spirit, whose face was that of Lora, and who could not sing as the little child did, because, though she was clad with joy as with a robe, in her eyes there was still a last lingering mist of human tears.

"And in Pharais, my bonnie," he would add whisperingly in the child's unheeding ear, "in Pharais there are no tears shed, though in the remotest part of it there is a grey pool, the weeping of all the world, fed everlastingly by the myriad eyes that every moment are somewhere wet with sorrow, or agony, or vain regret, or vain desire. And those who go there stoop, and touch their eyelids with that grey water ; and it is as balm to them, and they go healed of their too great joy : and their songs thereafter are the sweetest that are sung in the ways of Pharais."

Often Lora or Mary would be with him when he was thus speaking ; for each was fearful lest some day he should discover that his little *uan* was blind, and could never even open the sealed lids.

But on that last twilight of November, Alastair seemed to have been impressed by the passive stillness of the child, and to be troubled when he looked at it. He had kissed the eyes again and again, but they had not opened ; he had whispered loving words in the tiny ears, but they had not hearkened.

All that night he was restless, and rose often to look at the two sleepers in the bed opposite his own. Just before dawn, he looked for the last time. He was satisfied now. The little one smiled . . . but it was because that in the soundless, breathless passage from one darkness to another, it had heard a sweet voice at last, and at last had, with suddenly illumined eyes, beheld a new glory.

So white and still was it that, when the cold of the tiny hands against her bosom awoke Lora, she lay looking upon it for a while, rapt in a new and strange awe. Then, having aroused Mary, she went to Sheumais, and brought him in to the room. Mary had already waked Alastair, and he sat holding the small white body on his knees, stroking it gently.

When Lora told him that their baby was dead, and asked him if he knew what she said, he did not reply ; but a tear rolled down his cheek, and he put his hand to his heart as though to still the ache of his inarticulate pain.

But after Mary had read from the Book of Psalms, and prayed in a low voice, all rose and passed out into the sunshine ; and Alastair, already oblivious of his loss, went down by the shore, and smiled with pleasure at the leap and fall, and chime and whisper, and sweet, low laughter of the sunny waters.

About a hundred yards inland from the cottage, a gigantic pointed stone rises from out of the heather. It is known among the isles as Fingal's Bolt, though neither Fionn nor his son, Ossian, ever threw that huge, flat-sided, fang-like rock. A few rude lines and even letters are still discernible on the side next the sun ; but there is probably none who could decipher that old-world rune, carved in bygone ages by the hand of a Druid.

Of all places in the island, except the rocky headlands whose flanks were laved by the sea, this Stone of the Past, as Sheumais called it, was that most frequented by Alastair. At its base he had listened, as a boy, to the tales of the old islander ; beneath it, his fantasy now persuaded him, was one of the hidden ways that led to that House of Paradise of which he so often dreamed.

There the four silent mourners met that afternoon to fulfil the wish of one among them, who loved to think that his little *uan* would come back some moonshine night or in a still dawn, and, taking their hands, lead his father and mother by that secret pathway through *Domham Tòir* to *Tir-na-h'Oigh*, whence, in good time, they would arise and go up into Pharais.

Lora had already been on the spot

with Sheumais. While the latter had dug the place of sleep, she, with white chalk picked from the shore, had printed in large, heavy letters these words upon the seaward side of the stone :

"Take unto Thy compassion this little one, and us who follow."

There were no words spoken as Mary, kneeling, took the child from Lora's arms, and laid it, wrapped in a white sheet filled with fragrant gale, in the wood-shored grave that had been reverently prepared.

The afternoon had grown chill. Seaward, a grey mass had risen as if out of the waste of waters.

All were still kneeling—while Sheumais laid turf and heather above the small wooden lid covering the narrow house that would give the body sanctuary for a time—when the snow began to come down.

There was no wind, so the flakes fell light as feathers, grey in the gathering dusk as the down that falls from the wind-swept breasts of wild swans in their flight to or from the Polar seas.

Denser and denser it came ; soundless at first, but after a while with a faint rustling and whirring, as though the flakes were wings of invisible birds of silence.

The grey-gloom thickened. Already the sea was obscured. Its voice was audible the more loudly . . . a calling voice; but dull, listless, melancholy with ancient, unforgotten pain and all its burthen of immemorial lore.

The four mourners rose. The two women, with bowed heads, murmured words of prayer and farewell. Sheumais, crossing himself, muttered:— " Deireadh gach comuinn, sgaoileadh ; deireadh gach cogaidh, sith " — " the end of all meetings, parting ; the end of all striving, peace." Alastair looked eagerly through the snow-dusk lest the child should come again at once and go by them unseen.

By the time they reached home, there was a thick twilight all about them. A little later, looking out into the night, they saw the flakes drift over and past them like a myriad of winged things hurrying before a wind that pursued, devouring. The island lay in a white shroud. At the extreme margin, a black, pulsating line seemed to move sinuously from left to right.

Suddenly a deeper sound boomed from the sea, though no wind ruffled the drifts which already lay thick in the hollows. Till midnight, and for an hour beyond, this voice of the sea was as the baying of a monstrous hound.

None in the homestead slept. The silence, broken only by that strange, menacing baying of the waves as they roamed through the solitudes environing the isle, was so intense that sometimes the ears echoed as with the noise of a rush of wings, or as with the sonorous suspensions between the striking of bell and bell in monotonously swung chimes.

Then again, suddenly, and still without the coming of wind, the sea ceased its hoarse, angry baying, and, after lapse within lapse till its chime was almost inaudible, gave forth in a solemn dirge the majestic music of its inmost heart.

At last, after long vigils, all slept, though none so deeply, so unwakeningly as Lora.

Three hours before dawn the snow ceased to fall. An icy sparkle glittered league after league oceanward, as the star-rays pierced the heaving flanks and bowed heads of the sea-horses which had abruptly sprung up before the advancing ground-swell.

The cold was the cold of the Black Frost—bitter, sharp as a sword, nigh unendurable.

Shortly after dawn, Alastair awoke, shivering. He rose, threw some more peats on the fire; and then, having dressed and wrapt his plaid about him,

and softly opened and closed the door, ·
stepped out into the snow.

His breath caught with the cold, and
a greater weakness even than that
customary of late made him reel, then
lean against the wall for a few minutes.

Soon his faintness passed. The ex-
ceeding beauty of sunrise over that
vast stretch of waters, over the isle in
its stainless white shroud, filled him
with an exalted joy. Thereafter, for a
time, he walked to and fro ; sometimes
staring absently seaward, again glancing
curiously at his shadow—scarce more
insubstantial than he himself had grown
within the last month, and particularly
within the last few days—as it lay upon
or moved bluely athwart the snow.

After a brief space, a rapt look came
into his face. He turned, and gazed
expectantly at the door.

No one coming forth, he entered,
and, with a loving smile, crossed to
Lora's bed.

"Sweetheart . . . my white flower
. . . come. It is so beautiful.
Pharais has opened to us at last. I
can see the steps gleaming gold within
the yellow shine of the sun. Beyond,
I saw a mist of waving wings. Come,
Lora . . . Come !"

Cold and white was she as the snow.
Alastair bent, kissed her lips, but was

so wrought by his vision that he did not notice the chill of them, nor see the blue shadow in the pallor of the face.

"Ah, *mùirnean, mo mùirnean,* see, I will carry you," he murmured suddenly.

He stooped, lifted the beautiful dead body he had loved so well, and, staggering beneath the weight, half carried, half dragged it to the snow-slope beyond the door. Gently he placed Lora down. Then, going for and returning with a deer-skin, laid her upon it, and sat down beside her.

For a brief while, he waited patiently for her awakening. Then his eyes wandered again, now fixt upon the majesty of the sea, reaching intolerably grand from endless horizons to horizons without end ; now upon the immense dome of the sky, where, amid the deepest blue, high in the northwest the moon turned a disc of pale gold out of an almost imperceptible flush, and confronted the flashing, blazing sunfire that, in the south-east, moved swiftly upward.

Suddenly he leaned forward; his lips parted ; his eyes agleam with the inner flame that consumed him.

"Lora . . . Lora, my fawn," he whispered. "Look ! The gates are opening ! Dear, all is well at the last.

God has given me back to you. My trouble is healed. Speak to me, dear; too great is my happiness!"

No sound: no movement of the hands: no stir of the closed eyelids.

"Lora!"

It was strange. But he would be patient.

Idly he watched a small, grey snow-cloud passing low above the island.

A warm breath reached the heart of it, and set the myriad wings astir. Down, straight down above the isle and for a few fathoms beyond it, they fluttered waveringly.

The fall was like a veil suspended over Ithona: a veil so thin, so transparent, that the sky was visible through it as an azure dusk; and beneath it, the sea as a blue-flowing lawn whereover its skirts trailed; while behind it the rising sunfire was a shimmer of amber-yellow that made every falling flake glisten like burnished gold. The wind was utterly still; the sky cloudless, but for that thin, evanishing veil of dropping gold.

The sea lay breathing in a deep calm all around the isle. But, from its heart that never slumbers, rose as of yore, and for ever, a rumour as of muffled prophesyings, a Voice of Awe, a Voice of Dread.

CPSIA information can be obtained
at www.ICGtesting.com
Printed in the USA
BVHW060319231118
533517BV00014B/304/P